Winning Resources and Support

OU Business School

Book 1

Fundraising in Context

Prepared for the course team by Jane Isaacs, Jill Mordaunt and Terry O'Sullivan

COURSE TEAM

Dr Terry O'Sullivan, *Course Chair*

Barry Jones, *Course Manager*

Sue Treacy, *Course Team Assistant*

Sam Cooper, *OU Business School Regional Coordinator*

Joan Hunt, *OU Business School Regional Manager*

Amanda Shepard, *Institute of Fundraising*

Production Team

Simon Ashby, *Editor*

Paul Beeby, *Media Project Manager*

Martin Brazier, *Graphic Designer*

Holly Clements, *Picture research and Rights clearance*

Roy Lawrence, *Graphic Artist*

Gill MacIver, *Media Assistant*

David Richings, *Materials procurement*

Critical Readers

Sam Cooper, *Programme Coordinator*

Gail Devlin-Jones, *Eranda Foundation*

Chris Durkin, *University of Northampton*

Acknowledgements

We are grateful to the Institute of Fundraising for its assistance in the development of this course. The course team would like to acknowledge the contribution of the following authors whose work, ideas and creativity in previous courses have helped shape the thinking behind B625 Winning Resources and Support:

Julian Batsleer

Chris Cornforth

Jane Isaacs

Sarabajaya Kumar

Jill Mordaunt

Rob Paton

Alan Thomas

Sue Ward

The Open University
Walton Hall, Milton Keynes
MK7 6AA

First published 2007.

Edited and designed by The Open University.

Typeset in India by Alden Prepress Services, Chennai.

Printed and bound in the United Kingdom by Thanet Press Limited, Margate, Kent.

978 0 7492 2395 3

1.1

CONTENTS

INTRODUCTION TO BOOK 1

The theme of this book is to set the work involved in fundraising and campaigning in context. There are three, linked, levels on which we will do this: personal, organisational and ethical.

The first two sessions address the personal level. Session 1 looks at the kind of challenges fundraising provides to the people who undertake it. In spite of all the different things they do, there are some things which all fundraisers have to be good at (we call them 'core competences'). The activities in Session 1 give you an opportunity to think through these competences and how they relate to you.

Session 2 begins to develop the fundamental fundraising competence of planning, offering you some practical tools to help you plan, prioritise and manage your time on a personal level to maximise your contribution to the fundraising effort.

Session 3 addresses the next level of context for fundraising: the organisational level. Has it ever struck you how often there are tensions between the people who deliver services in organisations like charities and those whose job it is to raise the money to keep the organisation going? Session 3 explores these tensions and suggests ways of dealing with your co-workers as customers and stakeholders. It ends by explaining the process and value of branding to fundraising and campaigning organisations.

Session 4 introduces the third, and broadest, level of context for fundraising and campaigning: the ethical context. It looks at where charities and voluntary organisations fit into society, and explores the issues of ethics and accountability which are essential to maintaining their position of trust.

Book 1 has four main aims:

- to help develop your understanding of your role in your own organisation, and the competences you need to be effective in winning resources and support
- to provide you with some practical ways of planning, prioritising and managing your time in your work as a fundraiser
- to explore how fundraising approaches and activities fit into the wider organisational context
- to discuss some of the ethical issues and dilemmas involved in winning resources, and the role of regulatory frameworks and codes in promoting good practice.

Session 1

The Challenge of Fundraising

Session 1

CONTENTS

1 THE CHALLENGE OF FUNDRAISING

1.1 INTRODUCTION

The main aim of this course is to help you develop the competences that you need to be effective in winning resources and support. It starts in this session with a general look at the sort of work that is done in this area and the varied roles that fundraisers play both inside and outside an organisation. Most importantly, the session focuses on the key competences you will need to develop to be effective in your work.

Aims and Learning outcomes

This session has three main aims:

- to help you to take stock of your own experiences so far of winning resources and support
- to introduce a framework of competences which will be developed throughout the course
- to help you identify your own competences and those you would like to develop further.

After studying this session you should be able to:

- describe the different roles you may be expected to play when carrying out your responsibilities for winning resources and support
- describe the different clusters of competences necessary to be effective at winning resources and support
- make an initial assessment of your existing experience in this area and where you need to develop your own competences.

1.2 WORKING IN FUNDRAISING

'The principle of fundraising is to raise money by asking for it' (Institute of Fundraising, 2006b). While this description emphasises what all fundraising jobs have in common, the jobs come in a variety of forms, both voluntary and paid, to suit the needs of organisations and good causes that raise money and other kinds of support.

BOX 1.1

JOB ADVERTISEMENTS FOR WINNING RESOURCES AND SUPPORT

Durham Cathedral

Head of Development

Salary £29,000 to £34,000

Further details and an application pack are available from:

Mrs L Jeffrey,
Chapter Office,
The College,
Durham DH1 3EH
Tel: 0191 375 1220
www.durhamcathedral.co.uk

Closing Date for applications 23 January
Interviews will be held on 14 February

A recent BBC poll voted Durham Cathedral as Britain's best-loved building. Founded in 1093, it is a cultural and historical masterpiece, the shrine of St Cuthbert, the seat of the Bishop of Durham, and a living centre of prayer, pilgrimage and presence in north-east England.

The Cathedral is embarking on a Development Programme which will require money to be raised for its mission and its fabric. There will be opportunities to involve donors with a wide range of motivations and interests, including worship, music, visitor outreach, heritage and education, all in the context of an outstanding building at the heart of Durham's World Heritage Site.

The Cathedral Chapter wishes to appoint a suitably qualified fundraiser who will help to establish and lead a programme for the Cathedral's future development.

IISS

Director of Development

Highly Competitive Salary – London

"the world's leading authority on international security and political-military affairs"

A rare opportunity has arisen for an experienced and energetic Director of Development to lead the global fundraising strategy for The International Institute for Strategic Studies.

The Institute has an entrepreneurial culture and a committed and hard working staff that make, rather than merely grasp, opportunities.

The ideal candidate for this high profile position will have at least ten years of senior international fundraising experience. They will have outstanding networking abilities and the sensitivity required to manage high level donor relationships

The post is located at the organisation's headquarters in London, working closely with its offices in Washington and Singapore. A remuneration and benefits package commensurate with the skills and experience sought will be offered to the successful candidate.

The full job description is available at: www.darylupsall.com and more information about the IISS is at www.iiss.org

To apply please send us by email your CV and a covering letter to: recruitment@darylupsall.com

Interviews will take place in London, UK in early 2007.

Daryl Upsall
Consulting International

International Non Profit Recruitment Experts

New Marlowe Theatre, Canterbury

The Marlowe recast canterbury

CAPITAL DEVELOPMENT PROJECT

The Marlowe Theatre, located in the heart of Canterbury, is East Kent's flagship performance venue and one of the most successful theatres in the south-east, with audiences rising by 22% per annum for the last 5 years.

Canterbury City Council has recently made a decision, subject to the ability to raise sufficient external funds, to redevelop the theatre, creating a new centre of excellence for the performing arts, with a 1200 seat auditorium, a smaller studio space, café, bars, training and learning spaces, gallery areas and a new city centre piazza and riverside walk.

The estimated cost for this work is £23 million. The council will invest around £8 million and anticipates raising up to £9 million from other public sources. At least £6 million must be raised from trusts and foundations, private sponsorship, friends/patrons of the theatre and a public appeal. The Marlowe Theatre Development Trust will lead this part of the fundraising campaign.

We now wish to appoint an experienced professional fundraiser to co-ordinate and manage this big gift campaign. Based at the Campaign Office, the co-ordinator will be expected to operate successfully at both a strategic and 'hands on' level. This will include developing existing contacts and identifying and cultivating new funding opportunities.

Experience of a successful major capital campaign is essential.

Fundraising Campaign Co-ordinator

Three year contract £39,456 - £42,066 p.a.

The closing date for applications is **23 January 2007**. Interviews will be held in Canterbury on 2 February 2007. For a confidential discussion, call Janice McGuinness, Head of Culture & Communications on **01227 862 492.** To apply on-line, visit our website at **www.canterbury.gov.uk/jobs** or e-mail **jobs@canterbury.gov.uk** for an application pack quoting reference 1705. Alternatively telephone **01227 862 072** (24 hour answerphone).

We can supply application packs in Braille or large print format if required.

CANTERBURY CITY COUNCIL

DRAKE MUSIC PROJECT

'working with disabled people to make great music'

HEAD OF FUNDRAISING

£35K-£40K, full-time position, 6-month probation

the drake music project

Drake Music is the only national arts organisation delivering a wide range of music technology initiatives with disabled people of all ages. We now seek a pro-active and experienced fundraiser to devise and implement all aspects of Drake Music's fundraising programme, specifically around a major event in 2008 celebrating the charity's 20th anniversary, establishing a diversified sustainable income for the longer term. We would expect the candidate to have a successful track record in arts fundraising and to have a passion and commitment to the delivery of our services.

A senior management position based in London, you will lead on the charity's fundraising, support regional fundraising and potentially build a small fundraising team.

For further information, please contact Drake Music Project on 020 8692 9000 or visit www.drakemusicproject.org to download further details. To apply for the post, please send a CV, cover letter with statement clearly addressing the Job Description and Person Specification to Carien Meijer, Chief Executive, Drake Music, The Deptford Albany, Douglas Way, London, SE8 4AG.

Closing date: 12noon Friday 19th January 2007
Interviews will take place in London on Wednesday 24th January 2007

ARTS COUNCIL ENGLAND

Job Description – Fundraiser, Zambia

Job title: Fundraiser
Employer: Tikondane Home Based Foundation
Location: Chipata, eastern Zambia

Purpose of the role
Tikondane is helping the community care for men, women and children living with AIDS. Your role will be to raise money to support the activities of Tikondane. You'll be working to support fundraising activities from various donors, as well as building the capacity of support groups to develop income-generating activities. Your work will enable Tikondane to continue to provide support to the HIV/AIDS sufferers in the surrounding areas.

Job summary
- Develop fundraising strategies and identify new sources of funding
- Maintain and expand relationships with donors
- Implement and manage donor management systems
- Initiate and produce proposals for any new fundraising projects
- Develop communication materials
- Train and support staff in income generation strategies and funding development

Professional requirements
You'll have a degree in a related field and a minimum of 2/3 years relevant experience. You'll have significant understanding of proposal writing and reource mobilisation. With excellent communication skills, you'll be able to demonstrate a strong ability to manage relationships with a variety of donors, ideally in challenging circumstances. Experience of the management of donor administration is also essential. This placement is available to those who have considerable (5 years +) experience but no formal qualifications.

Personal requirements
- Excellent interpersonal skills
- Flexibility
- Self assured
- Team player
- Ability to work independently and unsupervised

Duration: 24 months

Package: Local salary, accommodation, flights, medical insurance, grants and training provided.

This is an example of a placement recently filled by VSO. We currently require fundraisers for similar roles in Ethiopia, The Gambia, Ghana, Kenya, India, Nigeria, The Philippines, South Africa and Zambia.

(Source: Voluntary Service Overseas 2006, http://www.vso.org.uk/volunteering)

(Sources: *Arts Professional* (2007); *Professional Fundraising* (2007)

Activity 1.1 gives you an indication of the range of ways in which organisations and individuals approach winning resources and support.

ACTIVITY 1.1

Look through the recruitment adverts and volunteer information in Box 1.1. On the face of it, they look very varied. Try, however, to think a bit more closely about the areas of similarity and difference between them.

Make a few notes below on what you see as the main similarities and differences between the jobs advertised.

Similarities:

Differences:

Some possible answers:

Similarities: All concern winning support and presenting the organisation and its message to potential donors or supporters outside the organisation; many are about acquiring resources; often they are a means to an end rather than an end in themselves; often the jobs don't involve working directly with the main groups the organisation has been set up to serve.

Differences: Some require specialist skills, some general; some involve work with colleagues as part of a team and some involve working alone; salaries and conditions of service differ – one is even a volunteer position.

Activity 1.1 highlights the fact that working in fundraising can be complex and varied. In some large organisations, the sorts of job activities listed in Box 1.1 may be undertaken by separate people, or even whole departments, each having a clear function and role in the wider work of the organisation. In small, informal community groups, however, this complex set of functions and roles may all fall upon a single member of staff with other, more general, responsibilities or an individual volunteer or management committee member.

Among the first things you will need to clarify, therefore, are:

1 the different sorts of *tasks* you have to undertake – and *roles* you have to play – in the course of your work

2 the *core competences* you need to draw on and develop to be personally and organisationally effective.

The remainder of this session will be an overview of each of these issues.

Now try Activity 1.2 which will help you assess your current work concerned with winning resources and support for your organisation or good cause.

ACTIVITY 1.2

(a) What are your main responsibilities in your current work? (Just list two or three – the most important ones.)

(b) Make a list of the main tasks you have to do in connection with these responsibilities.

(c) Which other departments or functional areas in your organisation do you collaborate with in carrying out these tasks?

(d) What proportion of your time do you spend on your responsibilities concerned with winning resources and support? (Is it a full-time job, or one of a number of things you need to juggle?)

1.3 YOUR TASKS AND YOUR ROLES

One way of looking at the distinctive features of your work is to consider the range of tasks you have to perform and the different roles you need to play in the course of your daily routines. A task is a piece of work with a beginning and an end. A role, on the other hand, is a continuous way of functioning which makes a distinctive contribution to a process, relationship or organisation. You have already made a note (in Activity 1.2) of the main tasks you perform. They are likely to involve you playing some or all of the following roles at one time or another:

Strategist – The environment in which you have to operate is changing rapidly. Organisations that rely on muddling through or doing what they have always done are in danger of being left behind. Increasingly, anyone with a responsibility for winning resources and support must be able to think strategically and take account of new opportunities and threats emerging in the environment.

Planner – The complexity of most campaigns to win resources or support demands careful planning. So you must be able to contribute to the planning process and make detailed arrangements so that things you say are going to happen do happen. This starts with the ability to plan and organise your own work.

Communicator – Communication is at the heart of winning resources and support. If you are going to win support for your cause you have to be able to communicate effectively and persuasively. You may have to persuade journalists of the merits of your cause, or donors that your cause is particularly worthy of support. It is likely that you will also need to be able to use a variety of media and choose between them as circumstances demand.

Manager and organiser – Staff and volunteers are often a vital resource in many forms of fundraising and resource winning. Their work requires organising, coordinating, supervising and supporting. So you may well have an important role in managing and motivating people.

Researcher – Effective fundraising is based on good research. If you want to apply to a trust for a grant you need to know which trusts are most likely to be sympathetic to your cause. If you are organising a direct mail shot you will be able to target this more accurately if you know something about the population you are aiming at. Developing research skills enables you to seek out, store and analyse information effectively.

Coordinator – Running a campaign to win resources or support means building and maintaining good relationships with a variety of individuals, groups and organisations. So you may have an important coordination and liaison role. Fundraisers need good links with the service providers in their own organisation so that they have a sound understanding of how the money they raise will be used.

Evaluator – The effectiveness of different methods and techniques for winning resources and support will vary according to changing circumstances. It is important to constantly monitor and evaluate the availability of different sources of funds and the performance of different techniques.

We should stress that these commonly encountered roles are not always clearly distinguished. They will not always be found as separate sections of your job description. They do, however, explain why – and how – in the course of your work you will have to act in a wide variety of ways.

Box 1.2 contains an extract taken from the diary of a regional organiser with general responsibilities for fundraising. Read it through and then tackle Activity 1.3.

BOX 1.2

SVEN'S DAY – A DAY IN THE LIFE OF A REGIONAL ORGANISER

1 Monday – caught the early train to Glasgow. Meeting to discuss draft plan for the organisation's 20th anniversary appeal. During journey sorted through in-tray I had picked up from office on the way to station. Sorted out items that needed urgent attention. One was a sponsorship deal I'd been trying to arrange with a local company. Another was an interview with a local reporter to publicise a new fundraising event with local schools. Telephoned her on the mobile to arrange a time later in the week. Then reviewed my work plans for the whole week – too much work and too little week! Prepared my thoughts for today's meeting. An important part of the plan was for house-to-house and street collections. Looked through statistics on the results of the last three collections in the region and comments of some of the area staff, to try to assess the feasibility of targets in the plan. They look ambitious.

2 Train late (again!) so arrived just in time to catch director of fundraising winding up her summary of the thinking behind the plan so far. Some of the regional organisers said that the targets being proposed were too ambitious given the current difficult economic climate. Also over confident about the number of volunteer collectors we could mobilise. Added my thoughts on this, backing up my argument with figures from previous collections. The director argued that the appeal targets were ambitious but realistic given that there will be a good deal of publicity about the 20th anniversary. However, she is expecting to discuss targets with each regional organiser in more detail.

Action point: prepare for that discussion.

3 Meeting then reviewed some of the written material for the appeal – too wordy and needs to be snappier; message not likely to appeal to younger people. Didn't feel this was really resolved but the agency working on this agreed to go away and see if they could sharpen up the copy. I raised some points about how to coordinate different aspects of the appeal between the centre and regions. Director listened and will email her response to all regional organisers by Friday.

4 Working lunch with director and regional colleagues. Discussion on the organisation's new strategy. Director reported back on her recent meetings with Trustees and senior colleagues, trying to convince them of the need for substantial investment in fundraising. She feels that income from trading is likely to be below target for at least 12 months. Also facing increased competition. She is convinced the organisation needs to invest now to secure necessary income in the future. But it's the usual uphill battle

convincing others! The very shortage of resources makes the Board less willing to spend money on fundraising. There had also been comments that fundraising ratios are declining. They don't seem to understand that during a period of investment this is bound to happen. I asked how the new strategy was likely to affect work in the regions and sounded the director out about a possible increase in fundraising staff in the region. She was a bit vague but said she had put plans forward for an increase in the next financial year.

5 After the lunchtime meeting headed back to the region. Train on time!! Picked up my car from the station then off to give presentation to an induction session for new volunteers.

Action point: PowerPoint presentation needs updating now we've adopted the Institute of Fundraising Code of Practice on Accountability and Transparency in Fundraising.

6 Finished the presentation at 7.30 p.m. Went well I think. One urgent message on my voicemail from Sunil (local organiser). A volunteer had had an accident while taking part in a sponsored cycle ride at the weekend. The press were raising questions about whether the event had been properly organised. Sunil had investigated the incident but wanted to meet urgently to discuss what approach should be taken. Phoned and arranged to meet at 10.00 a.m. the following day.

7 Home and checked email. Tomorrow is another day!

ACTIVITY 1.3

(a) Quickly look again at the activities described in Box 1.2. For each of the numbered paragraphs, identify the roles the regional organiser is playing.

1

2

3

4

5

6

You might have come up with the following:

1 *Planner – planning own work.*

Researcher/evaluator – looking up information to assess the feasibility of the targets.

2 *Planner – contributing to planning meeting.*

Communicator – communicating views on plan. (You may also have put the evaluator role down, as the regional organiser's contribution was based on an evaluation of past collections in the region.)

3 *Planner – contributing to planning meeting.*

Communicator – communicating views on plan.

Coordinator – trying to ensure coordination of central and regional plans.

4 *Strategist – considering the implications of the new strategy for the regions, and the possibility of more staffing.*

5 *Communicator – giving presentations to new volunteers. (You may also have suggested that this activity was part of the regional organiser's role as a manager.)*

6 *Manager – managing staff.*

(b) Now analyse your own activities in terms of the roles described on page 17. Start by noting examples of things you do that would fall under each of the roles. For example, under 'planner' you might put 'taking part in meeting to plan a mailshot to targeted donors', or under 'communicator' you might put 'contributing to a supporters' newsletter'. You may find it useful to go through your job description, look at last week's diary or this month's work plan, placing your various responsibilities under one or more roles.

Strategist:

Planner:

Communicator:

Manager/organiser:

Researcher:

Coordinator:

Evaluator:

(c) Which roles are particularly important and which are less important to you? It might help to give them each two, one or no stars depending on their relative importance. Write down the reasons for your decisions.

Strategist:

Planner:

Communicator:

Manager/organiser:

Researcher:

Coordinator:

Evaluator:

Which roles are important will depend a lot on the nature of your job. If you have general responsibilities for winning resources and support, then a number of roles are likely to be important. If you have a more specialist job then fewer roles are likely to be important. You may also have some discretion about which roles you develop most fully.

This diversity of roles and tasks highlights the importance of flexibility and adaptability – and the need to develop a capacity for living with a certain amount of uncertainty and creative opportunism in your daily work. As we will see throughout the course, the ability to follow several different avenues at the same time is often an important ingredient for success. By their very nature, these aspects of your activities cannot always be readily codified or pursued on the basis of past routines. Being opportunistic, seizing the moment, taking a calculated risk, chopping and changing are all sometimes necessary features of the work. However, as we shall also see throughout the course, this does not mean that you should not be systematic in your work – quite the reverse, in fact. The ability to combine creativity with rational analysis and a systematic approach is one of the main challenges of winning resources and support.

1.4 CORE COMPETENCES

Another valuable way of approaching the work you do is to consider it in terms of a set of basic skills and competences which you can draw on in a variety of organisational settings for a variety of purposes.

Competence is the ability to do something to a particular standard – in our case to the standard required to be an effective fundraiser. The things that all fundraisers need to be able to do we call 'core competences'. The main aim of this course is to help you develop the competences that you need to be effective. So the framework of competences described below also serves as an introduction to the rest of the course.

The competences can be grouped together into eight broad clusters:

1. *Plan, implement and review particular events, appeals or campaigns*, including identifying needs, setting goals, managing the planning process, thinking strategically, planning events, implementation and review – within an organisational context.
2. *Communicate effectively with a variety of external and internal audiences*, including identifying audiences, writing skills, using the media, presentational skills, persuasiveness and asking for resources in person.
3. *Manage staff and volunteers*, including recruitment, motivation, supervision, support, development, and working with groups and committees.
4. *Collect, analyse and manage relevant information*, including prospect research, developing and acquiring lists, market segmentation, storing, analysing and updating information.
5. *Develop and maintain effective relations with donors, supporters and other relevant agencies*, including understanding donor/supporter motivation, developing and sustaining donor commitment, hiring and managing consultants.
6. *Deal effectively with the commercial aspects of winning resources and support*, including costing projects and plans, tendering and negotiating contracts, trading, legal and tax requirements.
7. *Choose and apply as appropriate various approaches or techniques for winning resources and support*, including knowledge of a range of fundraising and campaigning techniques and skill in applying at least some of them, within an understanding of ethical principles and the external fundraising environment.
8. *Develop your own personal effectiveness*, including flexibility, the confidence and tenacity to be able to ask for resources and support and accept rejection when it comes (as a part of the job, not as a personal reflection on you), an awareness of your own abilities and limitations and how to make the most of them.

Remember that not all these competences will be equally relevant for you at the moment. It depends on the nature of your current role and the organisation within which you are working. Remember too that the competences are not just relevant to winning resources and support. For example, managing staff and volunteers is a competence you might use in a variety of different contexts. This also means that experience and skills you have gained elsewhere may be relevant to you now – don't underestimate their value.

We will now look at these areas of competence in more detail, and how they relate to the rest of the course. The following series of activities (1.4–1.10) provide you with an opportunity to consider how important they are in your job and to take stock of your existing skills and experience. Where you do not have direct professional experience of a particular area, think about an area of your actual experience which addresses the same kind of competences. For example, you might not have any experience of dealing with costing a project bid (see Activity 1.9) but you may well have experience of working out the cost of a particular course of action in some other context.

1.4.1 Planning, implementation and review

> 'To fail to plan is to plan to fail.'

Planning is about setting goals and working out what needs to be done to achieve them. We all do planning every day. For many activities, such as organising a night out at the cinema or getting the children to school on time, the planning is often done informally. However, other activities, such as developing an appeal or fundraising event, are too complex to be tackled in this way. You may need to discuss goals, research options and assess the resource implications. Usually you will need to produce a formal written plan to share with others.

There are different sorts of planning that take place within organisations. The most long-term and general plans are usually called *strategic* plans. They try to set out where the organisation is going in the next three to five, or possibly even ten, years. For example, your organisation's fundraising strategy might set out a goal for the amount of revenue it expects to generate in five years' time and outline how it expects this goal to be achieved. At the opposite end of the spectrum is *operational* planning. These plans are the most short term and detailed, and involve the planning of particular projects, events or tasks, such as a fundraising concert or street collection. Operational planning is the last stage before implementation, the all-important point at which a plan is put into action. Implementation involves managing people, resources and deadlines to achieve results

Monitoring and review are, respectively, checking that a plan is on track to achieve what it set out to do, and evaluating how successful it has been. Monitoring takes place during the implementation of the plan and allows for changes to be made if it is going off track. Review, on the other hand, is something that happens at the end of a plan. Did it achieve what it set out to do? If the outcomes were different from those intended, what lessons can be learned to improve things next time?

ACTIVITY 1.4

(a) What plans are you responsible for preparing?

(b) What other plans do you contribute to in your job?

(c) Is this an area you or your organisation may need to develop? Explain briefly why.

Your answers to this activity will depend a lot on your level within your organisation and what sort of organisation it is. If you work in a small organisation or at a senior level in a large organisation you are likely to be involved in planning at a strategic level. Whatever your position, you will be involved in developing operational plans. A problem often mentioned by people is lack of coordination, and sometimes conflict between different plans (for example, central plans for fundraising clashing with local plans). Another common problem is lack of time for monitoring and review.

1.4.2 Communication and public relations

Communication is at the heart of winning resources and support. You can't expect to influence people and win their support if you are unable to communicate with each other effectively. You may communicate with people directly or indirectly through media such as newspapers, television or your website. To communicate effectively it is important to look systematically at:

- what *messages* you are trying to communicate and why
- the different *audiences* you are trying to communicate with and what you know about them
- the *opportunities* your different audiences have to communicate with you
- the various *methods* of communication and media you might use and their appropriateness for your particular purposes

ACTIVITY 1.5

(a) List the main groups and individuals your unit or organisation communicates with in relation to winning resources and support.

(b) What methods are used by your unit or organisation to communicate with them (for example letters, telephone, direct mail, newsletters, presentations, meetings, websites, podcasts, email)?

(c) How do you find out their views and opinions?

(d) What aspects of this work are you involved with?

(e) Is this an area you or your organisation may need to develop? Explain briefly why.

Organisations are often quite good at developing a variety of methods of communicating with funders, donors and supporters. However, they are often less good at finding out their views about the organisation and what it is doing.

1.4.3 Managing staff and volunteers

In many organisations much fundraising takes place through the actions of other people. These activities range from things like street collections or sponsored events, involving hundreds of volunteers all over the country, to small, high-powered committees overseeing a campaign, and often leading the search for 'big gifts'. It is likely, then, that at some stage in your career your work will involve managing and working with staff and volunteers.

Managing people requires the ability to work with both individuals and groups and an understanding of motivation. At an individual level, competences in recruiting, selecting, motivating, supervising, supporting and developing people are important. At a group and team level an understanding of roles and of some of the common problems of groups and how they can be tackled is a real asset and the ability to delegate and coordinate work is essential.

ACTIVITY 1.6

(a) How does your organisation use staff and/or volunteers in winning resources and support?

(b) What is your role in managing these staff or volunteers? If you do not have direct experience of working with staff or volunteers to win resources or support, have you any other experiences of managing people that you will be able to draw upon? Jot down some examples below.

(c) Is this an area you or your organisation may need to develop? Explain briefly why.

Organisations vary widely in the extent to which they have salaried staff and in their use of volunteers. Even if you do not currently have responsibilities for managing people inside the organisation, you may find yourself managing relationships and working with consultants and specialist suppliers.

1.4.4 Collecting, analysing and managing information

Fundamental to many forms of fundraising is having information on your present and potential donors and supporters. This information may be factual, such as a postcode or a record of their past gifts to the organisation, or it may be more complex and subjective, based on personal knowledge of the donor, their motivations and interests. This information is valuable. The more you know about donors and supporters, the more carefully you can target appeals or campaigns.

Many organisations devote considerable resources to collecting, updating and analysing information about potential and actual donors, members and supporters. Database packages allow for ever more detailed analysis and cross-referencing. This makes more sophisticated marketing and targeting possible. Knowledge of the principles of information management is vital for anyone concerned with winning resources and support.

ACTIVITY 1.7

(a) What information does your unit or organisation collect on donors, funders or supporters?

(b) How is that information analysed, stored and kept up to date?

(c) How do you contribute to the collection, management and analysis of information?

(d) Is this an area you or your organisation may need to develop? Explain briefly why.

Some areas for development that people often identify are:

- *Information quickly dates, so our organisation needs to develop better procedures for updating information.*
- *Information is held centrally in our organisation, so it is difficult to access it if you are working in local areas.*
- *Our system is not flexible enough, so I would like it to be able to hold more information about donors and supporters and be able to analyse it in different ways.*

1.4.5 Managing relationships

A fundraiser's job does not just stop at attracting donors. The key to success is to build relationships with donors so that they continue to give, maintain their interest in the organisation and even get involved in other ways. Anyone involved in winning resources and support must therefore be skilled at developing and maintaining relationships – not only with external supporters and funders but also with internal colleagues and trustees or directors.

Successful relationships are based on mutual respect and understanding. You need to know what motivates your donors or funders and what they expect from your organisation in return for their support. For example, large donors may expect regular personal contact and reports on how their money is being spent.

ACTIVITY 1.8

(a) What, if anything, does your unit or organisation do to try to develop long-term relationships with donors and supporters?

(b) What role do you play in developing these relationships?

(c) Is this an area you or your organisation may need to develop? Explain briefly why.

Doing this activity may have made you reflect that relationships with individual donors and supporters are just one part of the network you need to nurture. Fundraising increasingly requires the collaboration of a range of different organisations. These relationships may be primarily commercial, as in the case of advertising agencies, direct mail operations or consultants employed by the organisation. Or they may mean partnerships with other similar organisations to run a particular appeal or campaign together. Much funding from government is linked to service agreements and contracts which specify formal monitoring and reporting arrangements. Knowing how to develop and manage a relationship with suppliers, consultants, contractors and partners – and get the best from them – is an important competence to develop.

1.4.6 Commercial competences

An ability to cost plans and estimate their likely returns is important if you are to be able to assess the feasibility of any campaign or project. There is often a temptation to under-cost projects or bids for contracts. People may believe they will increase their chances of raising money if they don't ask for too much. The result is that they get too little and are perpetually underfunded or in a state of crisis. A better strategy is to cost the project realistically, including money for contingencies and overheads, then spend time defining and redefining the case so that people will want to support your cause or project.

If your organisation is going to be able to bid for contracts it must have the capacity to prepare tender documents, which will contain detailed costings and appropriate measures of performance, be able to negotiate agreements and be aware of the legal implications of any contracts that are entered into.

Raising money through the sale of goods or services requires a good deal of commercial knowledge and skills. In this course we are only able to consider some of the major issues you need to take into account in assessing whether or not trading is likely to be an option for your own organisation.

ACTIVITY 1.9

(a) What activities in your unit or organisation require commercial competences?

(b) What contributions do you make to these aspects of your organisation's work?

(c) Is this an area you or your organisation may need to develop? Explain briefly why.

The growth of activities such as trading and commercial partnerships, and the culture of accountability which accompanies major lottery grants and government contracts has meant that these competences have become more important in many organisations.

1.4.7 Practitioner know-how: the knowledge and application of fundraising and campaigning techniques

There are many methods and techniques for winning resources and support, and many 'how-to' guides and sources of information about them. It would be unrealistic to expect you to become expert in using them all. However, you should have some knowledge of the range of techniques available; which ones are most relevant for you will depend on your organisation and your own particular job.

ACTIVITY 1.10

Look at the list of some of the different methods and techniques for winning resources and support.

(a) Mark with a tick those you have some working familiarity with.

(b) Mark with a star those you feel that you would like to become more familiar with or skilled in applying.

- auctions
- big gifts
- catalogue sales and mail order
- celebrity and gala events
- collection boxes
- contracts/service delivery agreements
- direct mail
- fêtes, fairs and festivals
- gifts of shares
- grants from trusts
- grants from agencies – e.g. government/National Lottery distributors/European Social Fund
- house-to-house collections
- legacies
- lotteries/raffles
- newspaper/magazine advertising
- selling services (such as training)
- shops selling second-hand/other goods
- sponsorship
- sponsored events and activities
- street solicitation for committed giving (also known as face-to-face or direct dialogue fundraising)
- tax-efficient forms of giving
- telephone fundraising
- website.

This is not an exhaustive list! Make a note of any other methods that you use or feel are appropriate for your organisation.

1.4.8 Personal effectiveness

There are various competences associated with personal effectiveness. Some of these, such as time management are common to a range of different management jobs and are dealt with only briefly in this course. Others, such as confidence, flexibility, the ability to ask for support, accept rejection and still come back in to work the following day, are vital for winning resources and support. Activity 1.11 should help you start to think about your own strengths and weaknesses in this area.

ACTIVITY 1.11

Try to answer the questions below. They relate to aspects of personal effectiveness and the sorts of activities you feel most comfortable with. Answer each question using the five-point scales shown.

	Not at all				**A lot**
Do you enjoy having direct contact with supporters and donors?	1	2	3	4	5
	Not very confident				**Very confident**
How confident do you feel in your abilities to deal directly with important donors or supporters?	1	2	3	4	5
	Very uncomfortable				**Very comfortable**
How uncomfortable/ comfortable do (or would) you feel asking a potential supporter for money or other resources face to face?	1	2	3	4	5
	Not very easy				**Very easy**
How easy do you find it to deal with the disappointment and rejection that often comes when a request for support is turned down?	1	2	3	4	5

You can use the analysis in Activity 1.11 to identify areas where you might need to develop assertiveness skills, or emotional resilience, in your work. Careful research and preparation before an important presentation or meeting can have a galvanising effect on your personal confidence, and becoming competent in other dimensions of your role reinforces your confidence across the board. Activity 1.12 gives you a chance to review your reflections on the competences which have occupied us for the past few pages.

ACTIVITY 1.12

1 Look back over the different competences discussed in this session. Then for each assess (a) how important each of the groups of competences are to do your job effectively; (b) how competent you feel you are already. Assess each on a five-point scale where 1 = not very important/competent and 5 = very important/competent. Record your assessment on the chart below.

		Not very important/ competent				Very important/ competent
Planning, implementation and review	(a) (b)	1 1	2 2	3 3	4 4	5 5
Communication and public relations	(a) (b)	1 1	2 2	3 3	4 4	5 5
Managing staff and volunteers	(a) (b)	1 1	2 2	3 3	4 4	5 5
Collecting, analysing and managing information	(a) (b)	1 1	2 2	3 3	4 4	5 5
Managing relationships	(a) (b)	1 1	2 2	3 3	4 4	5 5
Commercial competences	(a) (b)	1 1	2 2	3 3	4 4	5 5
Practitioner know-how	(a) (b)	1 1	2 2	3 3	4 4	5 5
Personal effectiveness	(a) (b)	1 1	2 2	3 3	4 4	5 5

2 Which areas do you think it is most important for you to develop? Explain your reasons briefly.

This activity should have helped you start to take stock of the competences needed for your job, and your own existing competences. This should give you an idea of the areas where you need to focus your effort when studying this course. You might want to take this into account when planning your study time. Remember, though, that this is only a fairly crude form of self-assessment, and it depends on your subjective judgements. Sometimes we are not very good at judging our competences. So you may find it useful to discuss the activity with other colleagues at work who have some knowledge of your strengths and weaknesses.

1.5 SUMMARY

Here is a summary of the main learning points from this session:

- Fundraising covers a wide variety of jobs (voluntary, paid, full and part-time) in a very diverse range of organisations. Different as these jobs are there are some things that all fundraisers need to be good at doing.
- When preparing to improve our skills, at fundraising or any other kind of work, it is helpful to think about tasks, roles and competences.
    - A task is a piece of work with a beginning and an end.
    - A role is a continuous way of functioning which makes a distinctive contribution to a process, relationship or organisation.
    - A competence is the ability to do something to a particular standard.
- Common roles played by fundraisers are: strategist, planner, communicator, manager and organiser, researcher, coordinator and evaluator.
- Effective fundraising draws on the following clusters of competences:

1. Plan, implement and review particular events, appeals or campaigns.
2. Communicate effectively with a variety of external and internal audiences.
3. Manage staff and volunteers.
4. Collect, analyse and manage relevant information.
5. Develop and maintain effective relations with donors, supporters and other relevant agencies.
6. Deal effectively with the commercial aspects of winning resources and support.

7 Choose and apply, as appropriate, various approaches or techniques for winning resources and support.

8 Develop your own personal effectiveness.

- Being aware of your strengths and weaknesses in each of these areas is a good way of preparing to consolidate what you are good at and using your studies to improve in areas where you are less confident.

Session 2

Planning for Success

CONTENTS

2 PLANNING FOR SUCCESS

2.1 INTRODUCTION

This session focuses on planning. It begins by looking at why planning is necessary for winning resources and introduces the concept of the *control loop*. It explores the different levels of planning in organisations, what is involved in making plans, who needs to be engaged in the process and how you might plan for the unexpected to happen. We look briefly at writing a formal plan and, finally, discuss how you can plan to make the time to plan in the first place!

Planning skills are essential to effective fundraising. Planning is a theme to which we will return several times through the course – for example in the context of organising and planning events, and in developing longer-term fundraising strategy. Introducing it this early indicates its importance and will hopefully encourage you to reflect on it as background to your work on the rest of the topics covered.

Planning skills are also essential to distance learning, as you are no doubt aware by now. So we hope that this session will help you to consolidate your study skills as well as develop your professional competence.

Aims and learning outcomes

The aims of this session are:

- to describe and illustrate the importance of planning to activities such as fundraising
- to explain the different levels of organisational planning
- to introduce the concept of the control loop
- to explain the nature of planning and why it is often a repetitive and inexact process
- to highlight the social as well as the technical aspects of planning
- to outline a practical format for a written plan
- to help you make time to plan.

After studying this session you should be able to:

- differentiate between the different *levels of planning* needed in organisations and how they relate to *hierarchies of purposes*

- recognise the main uncertainties that surround any planning process, and the value of *contingency planning* and *pilot studies* to reduce the risks involved
- design the operational planning process for a particular appeal, campaign or event with regard to:
  - who should be involved and in what ways
  - the timing of the planning process
  - the different sorts of information required
  - the iterative and 'untidy' nature of planning
  - the form that written plans should take
- recognise the importance of managing your time to create the space in which you can plan effectively.

2.2 PURPOSES AND PLANS

2.2.1 Why plan?

Planning is about doing the right things in the right way for the right reasons at the right time. If your task is simple you may be able to do your planning in your own head. However, the more people there are involved and the more complex the activities, the more important it is to have some kind of written plan which can help to guide and coordinate people's actions. Without a good plan you are likely to end up with confusion, mistakes and possibly disaster.

Robust planning is particularly important in winning resources and support, not least because many activities involve the public. If they go wrong they may damage the reputation and credibility of your organisation. Box 2.1 shows what can happen when planning is neglected or done poorly. Here is the text of a letter sent to a local newspaper.

BOX 2.1

AND THEY CALLED THIS FUN ...

I would like to express my total disgust at the lack of organisation on the recent sponsored bike ride. The sponsorship form stated: 'If entrants drop out it is vital they go to the nearest marshal to receive written proof of the distance completed'. We cycled for 15 miles before we saw the one and only marshal. 'Refreshments for riders would be supplied at the finish and at intervals along the route.' There were no refreshments around the route or at the finish. The total lack of markings along the route made it impossible to know where you were going – even the police didn't know. The sponsorship form said 'A Sponsored Fun Ride on the Redways'. Fun Ride? You must be joking. After cycling around in circles for two hours in pouring rain, would you call this fun?

I, for one, would not attempt this event next year.

So planning is about trying to reduce the chances of things going wrong and to increase your chances of success. Your plan should enable you to assess whether what you want to achieve can be done in the time and with the resources available.

2.2.2 Planning for control

Two ideas are fundamental here: *planning* and *control*. They are inextricably linked. Without a plan you have no basis for control and no reference points against which to assess your progress. Yet without monitoring and control, a plan is just a statement of aspirations and intentions. The 'control loop' diagram (Figure 2.1) captures the essential elements in the process of 'making things happen' and paying attention to the stages shown can help prevent many over-runs and crises.

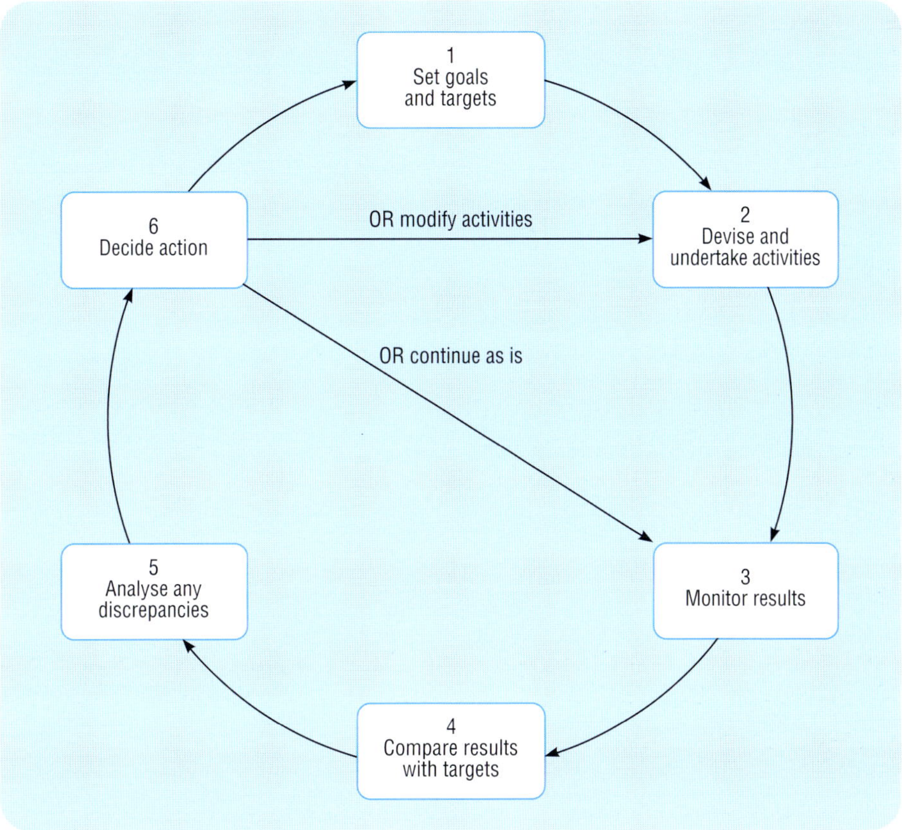

Figure 2.1 The control loop

ACTIVITY 2.1

Think about a recent fundraising activity (or event or campaign) which you were involved in planning, or identify one which you are planning at the moment. Now show how you could apply the different stages of the control loop to your chosen activity/event.

(a) Set goals and targets

(b) Devise and undertake activities

(c) Monitor results

(d) Compare results with target

(e) Analyse any discrepancies

(f) Decide action

How did you get on? Depending on your level of experience, your role and the size of your organisation, it may be that you have not been directly involved in all six stages. For instance, your goals and targets may have been set by head office but you have had responsibility for devising and undertaking activities to achieve them yourself, checking that they are going to plan, and making any necessary adjustments.

My answer to this exercise was based on the example of running a street collection for a local charity. We had an overall target amount to raise as a contribution to general running costs. The goal for this particular activity was based on what the charity had managed to collect in previous years as well as how many volunteer collectors we felt we were likely to recruit. The actions we devised and undertook included getting permission and a date from the local council, borrowing collecting boxes from another charity, putting labels and seals on them, ordering stickers from national headquarters to give donors, recruiting volunteers, organising the secure distribution and collection of the boxes and their contents, and finally banking and accounting for the proceeds. 'Monitoring results' consisted mainly of checking progress on recruiting volunteers as the date of the collection approached, and desperately phoning round to boost numbers. We were able to compare the resulting amount of money raised with the original target – something of a disappointment due to fewer volunteers than we had hoped for (another result to compare with target) and compounded by very poor weather on the day in question. Analysing these discrepancies made us seriously question whether the street collection was actually a viable activity for the following year (the last stage 'decide action'). Would our resources of time and people be better applied to something more lucrative and less labour-intensive? In the end, what decided the charity to repeat the exercise the next year was the feeling that a visible presence in the high street had advantages over and above the absolute amount of money collected (although whether some of the weather-beaten volunteers would have agreed is another question).

A number of writers and training courses in fundraising use a specialised version of the control loop model called 'The Fundraising Cycle' (Institute of Fundraising, 2006b). It summarises the stages of planning for any kind of fundraising campaign into four broad steps of (1) establishing a case for support, (2) research, (3) developing the plan, and (4) monitoring and evaluating. It is particularly relevant to fundraising as it emphasises the importance of research into potential sources of support before deciding what activities to undertake. We are using the more general model of the control loop here to introduce the concept of planning as it deals in greater detail with the actual stages of any kind of activity.

You may feel that chopping up a process into these discrete phases is somewhat artificial. Life is never as straightforward as this, and some of the stages described can seem to merge into one another. However, precisely because activities like fundraising are often a lot more complex than they first appear, a technique like the control loop can help you develop a sense of direction and priority in the midst of it all. Here are some other advantages of planning using a model like this:

- *It saves time later on by forcing you to consider what you need to do, and with what resources, to achieve your goal. For example, even something as apparently simple as a street collection needs a considerable amount of advance planning and co-ordination of people, equipment and systems.*
- *The stages of monitoring, analysing discrepancies and deciding action give you more control over events, and a chance to learn from your activities.*
- *The shape of the model, whether we call it a loop or a cycle, conveys the real nature of planning as an ongoing process where the results of any current plan feed into the preparations for the next.*

2.2.3 Levels of planning

Plans are made in relation to particular purposes: we plan for something. So we need to distinguish between the different sorts of plan that are required for different sorts of purpose.

People use a whole range of words to describe 'what we are trying to achieve' – for example, aims, objectives, intended outcomes, targets, goals, values, mission, purposes. For an organisation with a clear sense of direction, these different statements of purpose will fit together in a logical hierarchy, as shown in Figure 2.2. At the top of the hierarchy are those words that tell us why our organisation exists; below them are broad statements of what we are trying to do; and as we go down the hierarchy there are increasingly specific statements of how we will do things. Alternatively, we can work our way up: achieving the targets means meeting our objectives, which means we realise our aims or goals, which in turn contributes to our mission and expresses our values.

Figure 2.2 The hierarchy of goals

This pyramid of purposes is associated with the rough hierarchy of different levels of planning shown in Figure 2.3. One level of planning blends into another, so these terms are not entirely clear-cut. Nevertheless, the main focus at each level is different.

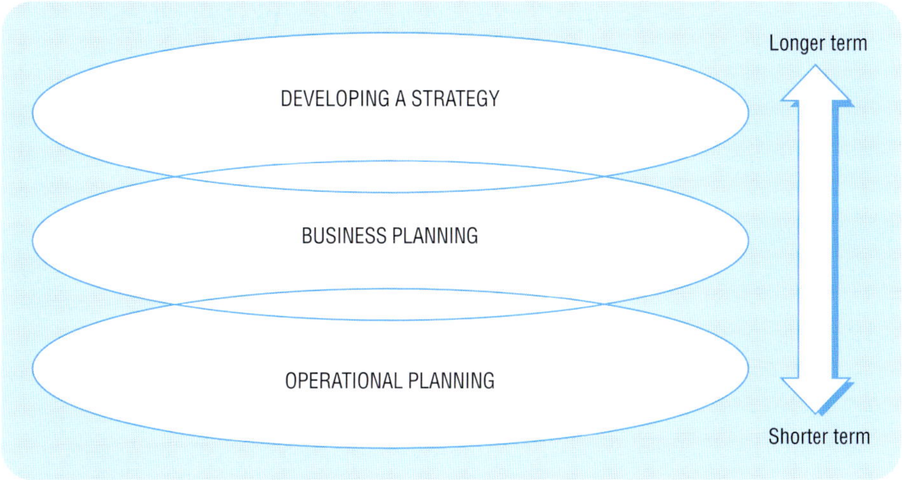

Figure 2.3 Levels of planning

While the focus in this session is mainly on operational planning, an understanding of all three levels will help you to understand how the different types of planning can work together within your organisation.

Strategic planning

The highest level of planning is called ***strategic*** planning. Strategy is concerned with setting out the *long-term*, *overall direction* of the organisation. Strategic planning involves:

- deciding how the organisation should respond to changes in the wider environment, and how it should position itself in relation to other organisations in the field
- defining the overall mission and goals of the organisation
- planning the long-term development of the organisation's activities, resources, structure and systems in line with these goals.

Strategic planning will have a profound effect on the goals and targets that feature in stage one of the control loop for lower-level plans. As the environment changes, so the opportunities and challenges facing the organisation will change too. For example, the YWCA (Young Women's Christian Association), which was founded in London in the nineteenth century, decided at the end of the twentieth century to refocus its work away from social housing for young women to youth and community projects instead. This new emphasis was seen as more relevant to the organisation's target group of service users, as well as being in keeping with the capability of the charity. A good way of understanding strategy is to see it as being about trying to obtain a reasonable match between an organisation's long-term mission and goals, the capabilities it has to carry these out, and the wider context in which it has to operate. This is illustrated in Figure 2.4.

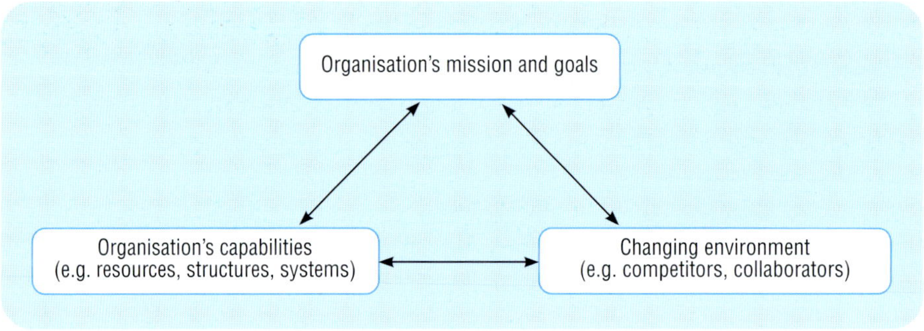

Fig 2.4 Strategy as a matching process

Sometimes strategy is not given priority in an organisation, perhaps because it is very young, having been set up to respond to an immediate and urgent need. Even in more mature organisations strategy can be implicit and taken for granted. Without a clear strategy different people may have different ideas about where the organisation is going. This may not be a problem in times of expansion but when hard choices have to be made the lack of a strategy becomes apparent. See Box 2.2 for an example.

BOX 2.2

COMRADES IN PEACE

Comrades in Peace was set up to provide support for veterans, retired soldiers, many of whom have now grown old and have significant health and social care needs. It runs three residential homes which cannot cater for those who need proper nursing care. The homes are becoming outdated and do not meet modern standards in terms of accommodation and facilities.

Over the years the organisation has come to rely on house-to-house collections, an annual appeal and a regular significant donation from a trust fund. However, it is now proving harder to recruit collectors, other appeals for 'younger' and more fashionable causes have been set up and the trust fund has recently reviewed its patterns of giving and indicated that it wishes to refocus its grant-giving onto children and young people.

The Executive Committee, advised by the new chief executive, wishes to close the residential homes and, with money from the land sales, establish a nursing home for those who are very frail, and offer home support services to others. The residents of the existing homes and their families are very upset about the proposals, which have been leaked to the newspapers. Each home also has an active and very influential 'Friends' group that runs local fundraising events and provide volunteer support. They are strongly resistant to the idea of change.

The new chief executive wonders why nobody saw this situation coming ...

ACTIVITY 2.2

Make brief notes on the following questions.

(a) To what extent does your organisation have a strategy for what it does and what it wants to become?

(b) How explicit is this strategy, and how widely is it understood and agreed?

(c) How has the strategy (or the absence or inadequacy of the strategy) affected your work?

(d) Broadly speaking, are there aspects of the strategy that are inadequate, or in need of revision or elaboration? For example, what new issues or opportunities or dangers are emerging?

(e) What are the obstacles to revising and clarifying the strategy in your organisation? What opportunities do you have for raising strategic issues?

The lack of an agreed strategy is usually shown up in difficulties and disagreements in planning and decision making (as in Box 2.2). Perhaps the most common obstacles to strategy formulation are preoccupation with day-to-day issues by senior staff ('fire-fighting') and major differences within the organisation over where it should be going (and hence the fear that raising fundamental questions will bring latent conflicts into the open).

Business planning

The core of a business plan is a forecast of income and expenditure over a specific time period or the life of a project. It is, in essence, a statement of how aspirations or commitments will be matched by resources. The plan sets out what it is proposed to do, and how much money will be needed, when, and from where it will come.

A business plan spells out the implementation of a strategy and demonstrates the feasibility of what is proposed, which is one reason why funding bodies often ask to see a business plan before making substantial grants or commitments. Business planning is also a way of thinking through the implications of different strategic possibilities. It converts the general principles and aspirations of a strategy into a quantitative forecast of activity and staffing levels, resource requirements and resource acquisition.

Operational planning

Operational planning is the day-to-day practical planning carried out by all of us in order to make things happen. It involves:

- clarifying or being committed to a particular goal or target
- identifying how, working with and through other people, it may be achieved within the given timescale and level of resources.

> This includes recognising necessary activities and who will carry them out, as well as provision for monitoring and adjustment.

It often appears less glamorous than planning strategies and developing business plans, but it is the vital preliminary to effective projects and day-to-day activities. At this level of planning you are dealing with the hard realities of tight timescales and limited resources. Therefore operational plans will usually be part of bigger plans. For example, a charity concert organised by a group of local volunteers may be part of an organisation's regional fundraising plan or linked to a national appeal (i.e. part of a business plan).

ACTIVITY 2.3

An organisation working on improving the environment in run-down parts of an inner city is part funded by a government agency and also by private-sector sponsorship. However, a reduction in government funding has now created the need for a major review within the organisation. The following matters have emerged and require action:

(a) The need to choose between two different major areas of the work of the organisation: work to renovate wasteland to create parks and playgrounds or work with schools on litter-picking and recycling. The cuts mean that funding is no longer sufficient for both areas of work and one or the other will have to go.

(b) An exciting looking new avenue of work has emerged, extending two or three years into the future in partnership with a private sector sponsor (part-funding only), but requiring significant input from the organisation.

(c) One site where work is at a very early stage has been identified by the Management Committee as a 'showcase' site. Given the urgency of the funding situation, they want the project there completed in three months (just possible) so that potential sponsors can be shown it as an example.

For each issue say whether a strategy, a business plan or an operational plan would be relevant and say why.

(a)

(b)

(c)

For (a) a strategy would consider each of these two areas of work and how they relate to the values of the organisation, its strengths and perceptions about the future – of both the organisation and the environment in which it operates.

For (b) you might consider that a business plan would provide a reasonably sound basis for assessing the idea. (There may also be elements of strategy here, in terms of how this would 'fit' with the strategic direction of the organisation.)

In (c) you would require an operational plan.

2.3 THE PLANNING PROCESS

2.3.1 What's involved in planning?

This section examines in general terms what is involved in preparing a plan for an appeal or campaign. If planning is about setting goals and working out what activities and resources are needed to meet them, then your plan has three main components:

1 various *goals and targets* to be achieved

2 a specification of the various *activities* that need to take place to achieve these goals, in what order and by when (including plans for monitoring and control)

3 an estimate of the *resources* likely to be needed to carry out these activities.

So, first set your goals, then decide how you will achieve the objectives and targets that make up the goals, and finally examine the resource implications. Of course, it is not quite this simple, because in reality goals, activities and resources are *interdependent*. Often we do not have a free hand to set the goals of our plan and any that are set have to take into account the resources that are likely to be available. Equally it will not be possible to work out the resource implications of any plan without a reasonable idea of the sorts of activities that will be necessary to achieve our goals.

What this means in practice is that planning is not a tidy, sequential process. You may need to try out different combinations of goals, activities and resources until you find what looks to be the most promising way forward (see Box 2.3 for an example). Another way of saying this is that planning is an *iterative* process. It involves a number of passes or iterations which progressively clarify goals, confirm what activities are needed and in what order, and determine what resources will be required. Through this process you refine your plan from a general idea to a well worked-out proposal with clear goals and targets, a schedule of activities and tasks, staff allocation, budgets, and so on. Along the way you will consider a variety of options. Some of them you might discard, perhaps because they turn out to be too expensive or too risky. You may develop and modify others to take account of new information.

BOX 2.3

THE SPONSORED SLEEP-OUT

An organisation working to support homeless people in developing countries planned a weekend sponsored 'sleep-out', designed to raise the profile of the organisation and the issue and to generate funds for a particular project. Their fundraiser's original plan was to have two sites – one in the main square in the city centre and the other on the campus of a local college. When the volunteer support group met, it became apparent that there were not enough stewards available to run two sites over a weekend, so the decision was made to focus on getting a larger turnout for just one night. A few days later – fortunately before the publicity leaflets were printed – a popular local band offered to give a free concert. This would generate more publicity – and attract greater numbers of participants – so it was decided to go for just one location. The fundraiser negotiated with the college that they would provide the power supply for the band and also make their sports hall available in case of rain. For the college it was a way of raising their profile in the community and for the organisation it increased both the potential publicity and the fundraising.

ACTIVITY 2.4

(a) Think of a recent occasion when you were involved in planning something important (either in a professional or a personal capacity). Can you apply the idea of iteration to the planning process you went through?

(b) Give an example of one of the iterations that you went through.

The 'sponsored sleep-out' story is a good example of how plans evolve to suit circumstances. Perhaps there are parallels between that story and the planning experiences you have drawn on to answer this activity. Did your iterations involve other people? One of the advantages of planning in a group is that iteration can take account of fresh perspectives and new information from other people to improve on the original plan.

2.3.2 The who, how and when of planning

So far this session has concentrated on planning as a largely *technical* process. However, planning is also a *social* process. It is no good developing a plan that only has *your* commitment to making it happen. Planning must stimulate and develop the involvement, contributions and commitment of a range of different people inside, and possibly outside, the organisation. Key considerations are:

- Who is to be involved in drawing up the plan?
- How will the plan be approved?
- How should the planning process be timetabled?

We will look at each of these issues in turn.

Who should be involved in planning?

Deciding who should be involved in the planning process is often a difficult balancing act. Involve too many people and the process is likely to be very long and costly. Involve too few people and you may miss vital information or meet unexpected resistance or disagreement when you come to implementing the plan. There are no easy answers to such dilemmas: you will need to use your own experience and judgement. As a starting point you might think about:

- Who will *implement* the plan?
- Who will be *affected* by the plan, and how directly are they affected?
- Who has *information* or *experience* relevant to the plan?
- Where is *resistance* to the plan most likely to come from?
- Who will need to *approve* the plan for it to gain legitimacy and support within the organisation?

In this respect planning together is about winning the *internal* resources and support you need to carry your plans forward.

In a fundraising context many activities rely for their success on the involvement of volunteers, for example in an appeals committee or a local fundraising group. Involving key volunteers in the planning process is an important way of building relationships, and developing commitment and motivation.

ACTIVITY 2.5

Consider a plan that you have recently been involved with preparing and/or putting into practice.

Who was involved in (a) formulating; (b) approving; (c) implementing the plan?

(a)

(b)

(c)

What means were used to involve people, such as meetings or commenting on drafts (if it was a formal written plan)?

Do you think these arrangements were adequate? If not, how do you think they might have been improved?

Who else do you think might have been involved in the plan?

What difference might their involvement have made?

A common problem is that those involved in implementing the plan are not adequately involved. This may mean that aspects of implementing the plan are unrealistic. This may cause problems and lower people's commitment to the plan (often referred to as 'ownership').

Gaining approval for the plan

A key consideration in formulating any plan is who has authority to approve or reject it. If you work in a small voluntary organisation it is likely that any plans will need to be agreed by the organisation's management committee. In larger organisations the process may be more elaborate and a number of individuals or committees may have to agree aspects of a plan. This consideration is also likely to affect the timing of your planning – for example, the management committee or appeals committee might only meet quarterly. Missing a key meeting might lead to damaging delays. You will need to be clear about these constraints at the start of the planning process.

Timetabling the planning process

In thinking about timetabling the planning process in an organisation, three important factors to consider are:

- *When people can be involved*: the planning process needs to allow time for the different groups that need to be involved to make their contributions. For example, if you need to consult members or volunteers time must be allowed for this.
- *The committee cycle* may provide important deadlines when certain aspects of the plan have to be discussed and agreed.
- Perhaps most important are any *critical deadlines* when aspects of the plan need to be implemented. For example, if you are organising a street collection or a fun run, how much notice must be given to the relevant authorities? It is no good developing the most wonderful plan if you leave yourself and your organisation insufficient time to implement it effectively.

This last point raises another important issue: when do you move from planning to implementation? Planning, particularly if it involves a lot of people, is costly in terms of time and resources. Knowing when to stop is difficult. So how do you know when a plan is good enough? Unfortunately there are no simple answers. At some point people who are involved in implementing the plan may feel that they have enough guidance to get on with the task of implementation. Or you might compare the plan with other similar plans that have been successful in the past to see if the level of detail is comparable.

Often time constraints will just force you to stop and get on with making your plan happen. Remember as well that plans don't have to be perfect! If you are working your way round the control loop by monitoring the implementation of the plan it will be possible to make alterations and refinements if you find that things are not working out as expected.

2.3.3 Recognising and coping with risks

Some options are likely to be riskier than others, but no course of action can be guaranteed to be a success. So an important aspect of planning is to identify what the main risks associated with any plan are and to try to work out what to do if things go wrong. This is often called *contingency planning*. If you are developing a new or particularly risky initiative it is good practice to run a smaller-scale pilot project first to test out the feasibility of your plan and to try to identify and iron out likely problem areas. For example, if your organisation were launching a new advertising campaign it might well want to test the advertisements on a sample of people first to see how they respond.

Your plans may also involve financial risks, or risks to people. For example, what will happen if you are organising an open-air charity concert and there is bad weather? It may be that you can make alternative arrangements. If this is difficult, it may be possible to take out *insurance* to reduce financial risk. Or it may be possible to get the costs of organising the event sponsored so that your organisation will not lose if the event fails for any reason. The greater the resources that you are committing, the more important it becomes to assess these sorts of risks systematically and build contingencies into the plan to cover different eventualities. You will never eliminate risk entirely, but with good planning you should certainly be able to reduce it, and know what your maximum loss could be.

The ever-present nature of risk also highlights the importance of building arrangements for *monitoring* and *reviewing progress* into your plan – back to the control loop again (Figure 2.1). If you don't have a means for regularly monitoring the implementation of your plan and the results it is achieving you won't know whether things are going as intended. If you know what is happening you will be in a better position to take corrective action if things go wrong. Equally you will have an opportunity to learn from your experiences.

ACTIVITY 2.6

'Bullet proofing' is a way of identifying the parts of your plan which are particularly vulnerable and where there might be serious implications if things go wrong.

Thinking again about a recent plan you have been involved in drawing up, list some of the assumptions you made in creating your plan (for example, minimum number of tickets that will be sold, expectation of fine weather, etc.).

1 ____________________

2 ____________________

3 ____________________

4 ____________________

5 ____________________

6 ____________________

Now apply the following questions to each assumption:

(a) How likely is the assumption to turn out false?

(b) If the assumption does turn out to be false, how serious will the resulting problem be?

Now you can place your answers in a bullet-proofing table (Figure 2.5).

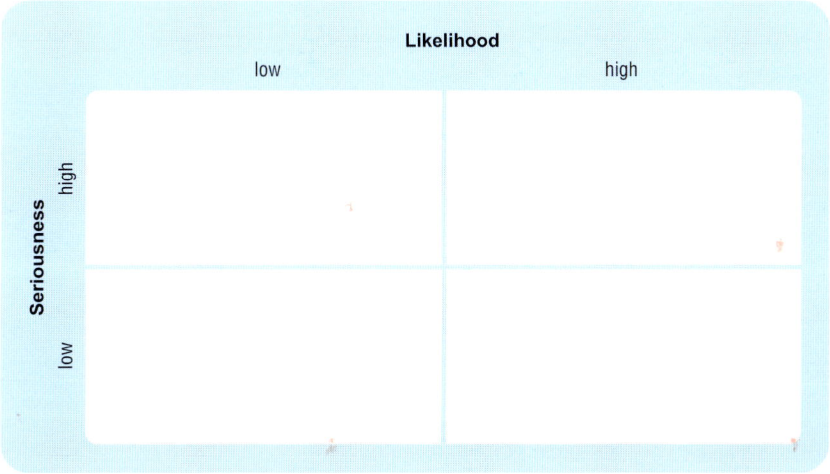

Figure 2.5 Bullet-proofing table

The table shows the results of your analysis in an organised way. You may want to think about preparing responses to the possibilities you have identified – or at least to those that fall into the top right-hand box – high likelihood/high seriousness.

2.4 YOUR WRITTEN PLAN

So far this session has concentrated on the process of planning – why it is necessary, what is involved in planning, who should be involved, timetabling, and so on. In this section we will concentrate on the contents of a plan and what a written plan should look like.

If your plan is complex or has to be communicated to a number of people, then almost inevitably you will have to present some sort of written plan. Although you may regard this as a chore, it is a useful discipline. Writing the plan is where a lot of the planning actually gets done.

Remember that a written plan is a crucial *communication* device. It is a way of letting everyone involved with the plan know what is happening, what is expected of them and how what they are doing fits in with other people's initiatives. It needs to have a clear structure and be clearly written. Box 2.4 outlines a possible structure for a written plan and summarises the sort of content that it should include. You do not need to follow this structure exactly in writing your own plans, but it does give a good indication of the sorts of things that should be included.

BOX 2.4

AN OUTLINE FOR A PLAN

Summary

If the plan is of any length it should have a brief one- or two-page summary at the beginning outlining the most important points – *what* you intend doing, *why* it needs to be done, *how* you intend to do it, and *when* it will be completed. This will act as an overview of the plan for those who do not have time to read it properly, and a reminder of the key points for those who do.

Introduction

This should outline the reasons why the plan was prepared, and introduce the rest of the report.

Background analysis

This section summarises your analysis of the current situation and the reasons why you are putting the plan forward. You may want to outline other options that were considered and why they were rejected. It is also important to show how your plan fits in the wider context, for example how it fits in with other departments within your organisation, or with the external environment.

Purpose of the plan

This sets out the main goals of the plan and how you think they will be achieved. These should be set within the context of your unit's or organisation's wider goals.

Action plans

These set out the lower-level objectives and tasks that have to be achieved and how this will be done. Action plans often consist of an ordered set of activities to be done. In addition it is important to know *who* will do them, and by *when*. This information is often contained in schedules.

Contingency plans

This outlines what the main risks associated with the plan are, and any contingency plans that have been developed to deal with these risks if things go wrong. It should specify the steps taken to reduce unavoidable risks, and what insurance provisions have been made, if applicable.

Managing implementation

This outlines how the process of implementing the plan will be managed. In particular it is important to detail how implementation will be monitored and the arrangements needed to alter or adjust the plan if it does not work out as expected.

Evaluation

This will discuss any arrangements that have been made to review the success of the plan. You need to explain what criteria you will use for success, and how you will measure it. These criteria should relate directly to the objectives you have set.

Resource implications

This sets out what resources will be required to carry out the plan. This information is often set out in budgets and staffing plans.

Appendices

These are a useful place to put detailed analysis or other technical data that the plan makes use of, so that the reader is not overwhelmed or distracted by information.

ACTIVITY 2.7

Look again at a plan you have written or, if you are new to preparing plans, get hold of one that has been produced in your own organisation. Read it through quickly.

(a) How well do you think the plan communicates what needs to be done and why?

(b) Do you think the plan is well structured?

(c) Is there other information that you think should have been included in the plan?

(d) How could the plan be improved?

2.5 MAKING TIME TO PLAN

This session has been all about planning. Agreeing that planning is very important is one thing; actually finding the time to do it is another. If you are busy and under pressure, planning can seem like a luxury that gets in the way of 'the real job'. You may find it difficult to get the uninterrupted time and space that you need to think things through. There is always another urgent task in the in-tray. All too easily this can become a vicious circle. If you can't make time to plan, then more often problems and crises will arise that demand your immediate attention, which makes it more difficult to find the time to plan!

As ever, there are no easy answers to this problem. However, recognising the nature of the problem and its causes is half the battle. A number of disciplines are useful in making sure planning does not get overlooked. You might want to try some of these approaches:

- Build time in at the beginning of all new projects and events for planning.
- Use the discipline of regular meetings, with staff colleagues or volunteers, to help construct and monitor plans.
- Make sure you put some time aside, perhaps at the beginning or end of the week, to plan your work for the following week. You could even try setting up a regular 'meeting with yourself' in your diary to protect your time to do this.
- Have a checklist of your longer-term objectives – say over the next six months. When planning next week's work, refer to the checklist and see how this relates to your longer-term objectives.

ACTIVITY 2.8

(a) What constraints limit the planning you can do?

(b) What actions can you take to help overcome these constraints, using the approaches outlined above?

2.6 SUMMARY

Here is a summary of the main learning points from this session.

- Planning is a technical and social process. The aim is to do the right things in the right way for the right reasons at the right time.
- Planning and control are inextricably linked.
- The control loop is a useful guide to the way plans develop in practice. It breaks the planning process down into six stages: setting goals and targets; devising and undertaking activities; monitoring results; comparing results with targets; analysing any discrepancies; and deciding action. Such action may consist of modifying activities in the light of the analysis, or continuing as is.

- The fundraising cycle is a version of the control loop summarising the main stages of a fundraising campaign as (a) establishing a case for support, (b) research, (c) developing the plan and (d) monitoring and evaluation.
- Planning in organisations involves a hierarchy of strategy (long-term direction), business planning (determining income and expenditure over a specific time period or project) and operational planning (the day-to-day practical planning which makes things happen).
- Planning is an iterative process between the three elements of: goals, the choice and specification of activities to achieve them, and the likely resources required.
- Planning as a social process needs to involve *who* (the relevant people), *how* (internal approval opportunities) and *when* (external deadlines).
- All plans carry risks. Contingency planning helps minimise threats to a plan by anticipating and monitoring risks.
- Bullet-proofing is a way of identifying and categorising risks by mapping them against the dimensions of how likely they are to occur and how serious their consequences might be.
- The more complex a plan is, and the more people it involves, the more important it is to have a written plan.
- An effective written plan might have the following elements (depending on the time and resources available, and the complexity of the project in question):

  Summary

  Introduction

  Background analysis

  Purpose of the plan

  Action plans

  Contingency plans

  Managing implementation

  Evaluation

  Resource implications

  Appendices.
- Planning takes time, which needs to be built into project schedules as well as your personal work routine.

Session 3

The Organisational Context

Session 3

CONTENTS

3 THE ORGANISATIONAL CONTEXT

3.1 INTRODUCTION

Relating your fundraising role to the wider organisation is the purpose of this session. In some organisations, perhaps a volunteer (who may or may not also be a member of the governing body) has taken on the resource-winning role and everyone else has heaved a sigh of relief and left them to get on with it. For others, focusing on fundraising can be an ongoing problem and many chief executives of smaller organisations can find themselves caught in the uncomfortable position of fundraising for their own job.

However, those organisations with a dedicated fundraiser or bigger ones with a substantial separate fundraising department may find that tensions and dilemmas emerge around the place of resource-winning and its relationship to the wider organisation. These tensions are also likely to be present in smaller organisations – perhaps not as evident as organisational issues, but more ones of role conflict. Teasing out what are effectively organisational tensions is useful in understanding why some aspects of fundraising are difficult to achieve. This session will help you to explore some of those tensions, particularly as they relate to organisational purpose and image.

Aims and learning outcomes

This session has three main aims:

- to explain how the activities associated with winning resources and support fit into your own organisation
- to show how the image or brand of your organisation is created from its mission and values
- to consider the implications of your brand for your fundraising and for how you represent your clients or service users.

After studying this session you should be able to:

- explain where the activities associated with winning resources and support fit in your own organisation and its wider context
- recognise the different factors that make up your organisation's image or brand.
- understand the issues involved in changing or developing your organisation's image
- contribute to thinking on how clients/service users are represented within your fundraising materials.

The session has three main sections. First, it looks at the place of winning resources and support in organisations and offers a framework for identifying those you need to build relationships with. Who are your main stakeholders or customers for your activities, both internally and externally? Second, it examines the concept of organisational image and how this might relate to some commercial sector ideas about branding. Third, it looks at the challenges involved in changing or developing your organisation's image. Finally, it discusses some of the issues about how those who use your services are represented in fundraising campaigns.

3.2 RELATIONSHIPS INSIDE AND OUTSIDE

Resource-winning activities are central to enabling an organisation to achieve its goals and, indeed, to secure its very survival. Without resources the organisation will quickly die. But relationships with other parts of your organisation and the wider environment can throw up all sorts of concerns about fundraising. At times it may appear that your work is viewed as a regrettable necessity or even not part of the *real* work at all. Sometimes you may feel that your efforts are undervalued. Perhaps colleagues in other departments are unwilling to acknowledge your professional expertise and the significance of your distinctive contribution to the organisation, or you attract the criticism that your activities are in some way undermining the values and principles of the organisation. Sometimes it may even be alleged that the requirements of funders may take priority over the needs of your service users in a way which threatens to distort the mission of the organisation.

How you are seen by the rest of your organisation and the wider environment in which you operate depends on the relationships you build with them, but there may be tensions and ambiguities that are not of your making. Different people may have not only differing interests in what you do but also differing views about how you should do it. Understanding how you relate to all the diverse expectations of your role will help you to see where the tensions and conflicts may arise and to adopt strategies to address these, if not resolve them. In order to do this you need to have some understanding of the various audiences for your performance as a fundraiser. So we now turn to a brief discussion of stakeholders and customers to see if these concepts can assist your analysis of your work and your role.

Stakeholders and customers

You are probably familiar with the term 'stakeholder'. A stakeholder is any person or group that has a legitimate interest in an organisation and what it does, and the capacity to affect it. For example, staff, funders, volunteers, supporters and beneficiaries are all stakeholders. But have you thought about the implications of the differing stakeholder maps for different sectors?

Consider the diagrams in Figure 3.1.

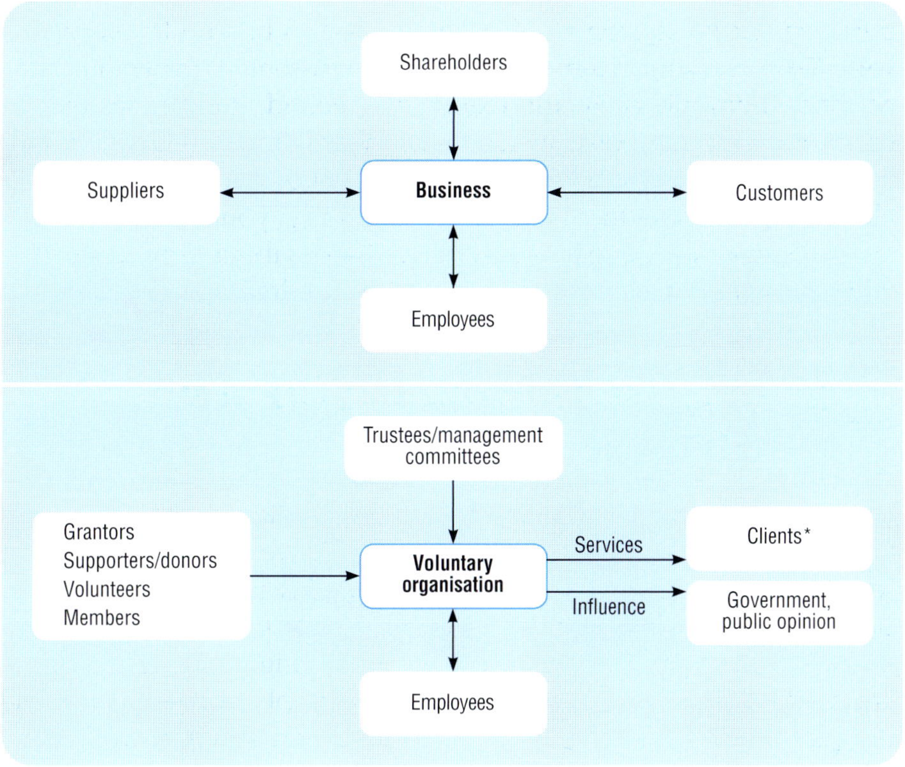

*Note: Where voluntary organisations make a charge for services, clients will also be contributing income to the organisation and may increasingly see themselves as customers.

Figure 3.1 The main stakeholders of typical business and voluntary organisations

Did you notice the different flows of inputs and outputs as illustrated by the direction of the arrows? In private-sector organisations there is a 'bottom line' of profitability. Organisations will only produce what can be sold profitably *and* generate returns for owners or shareholders. Such organisations have a close relationship with their customers and they will happily produce more and more of what their customers demand and will pay for. Voluntary organisations have a less straightforward flow of inputs and outputs, as is clear from Figure 3.1. This creates the following sources of tension which go some way to explaining the range of attitudes to the fundraising role within an organisation:

1 The lack of relationship between those who supply the resources and those who consume them. If, for example, you are providing services for homeless people, you can only provide the amount of service for which there is funding no matter how much the demand from homeless people increases. This can lead to stress and burnout for project staff, who may have to make heartbreaking decisions about who does or does not receive your help. This in turn puts pressure on you as a fundraiser.

2 The fact that non-profit organisations do not have owners in the same sense as private-sector organisations. Voluntary organisations generally have a governing body that represents the interests of the beneficiaries and hold the organisation 'in trust' for them. Usually in the UK these people are known as *trustees* and there are very clear laws about the financial relationships they are allowed to have with the organisation.

As a fundraiser you are accountable to this body, but you also need to ensure that no breaches of the law take place.

3 How voluntary organisations talk about what they do. As is clear from Figure 3.1 the fundraising role focuses on the 'inputs' into the organisation. It is a means to achieving the ends – or outputs – of the organisation: the *cause*, the *service*, the *campaign*, or, in some cases, the *maintenance* of the organisation itself. The distinctive values and purposes of the organisation are invariably framed in terms of those ends/outputs. This means that your contribution to the organisation can often be seen as subsidiary and rather instrumental. Providing the service or furthering the cause are seen as 'the real work' of the organisation; your work, while being entirely necessary, can nevertheless be overlooked.

4 The fundraiser's own perspective on the organisation. Many voluntary and public organisations find it hard to acknowledge the legitimacy of the interest and stake of donors and other funders in the work of the organisation. They hold themselves accountable instead to clients and users in the wider community. Because fundraisers have such close and regular contact with funders and donors, their perception of the work of their organisation may differ from the perceptions and commitments of colleagues who are either general managers or who are involved mainly in direct service provision. Your particular external orientation is inevitably reflected in your internal working relationships with other colleagues and sections.

5 Conflicting expectations. The fact that fundraising and resource acquisition require those involved to look in different directions from those responsible for service delivery can give rise to conflicting demands and expectations. On the one hand, you are expected to be effective and successful in your own terms. On the other hand, you are required to adhere to the dominant culture of the organisation – and not to undermine it by the working methods you adopt or the groups you work with. Think of a fundraiser working in a conservation organisation, for example. Fundraising is likely to get best results from focusing on attractive animals and issues which catch the public imagination – for example pandas, elephants, the exotic wildlife of the rainforests. People working in conservation say that the issues are far more complex and there should be far more emphasis on topics such as habitat management.

ACTIVITY 3.1

(a) List the main stakeholders you and your unit or organisation are involved with.

(b) Note down what you think are the main expectations each of these stakeholders has of your unit or organisation.

(c) Make a note of any dilemmas you are currently aware of arising from these different sets of expectations.

Some common dilemmas that people have raised are:

- *Funders having a different view of the value of the organisation's services from other stakeholders, and the danger of becoming funding-led.*
- *Balancing the need to present the organisation in a way that will be attractive to donors, perhaps by using emotive stories, and trying to 'educate' people about the work of the organisation.*
- *The public expecting fundraisers and campaigners to be expert in all aspects of the organisation's work yet other departments being reluctant to involve them in their work.*

As you must be getting used to hearing by now, there is no quick fix for these dilemmas. The purpose of thinking about stakeholders and their interests in this way is to help clarify some of the underlying causes of tensions around the fundraising role and how it is seen in organisations. Armed with this understanding, you may find it easier to manage your internal and external relationships more effectively.

Another way of thinking about your audience is as *customers* and *suppliers*. You may think that a word like 'customer' simply means someone who goes into a shop to buy something and that this is not a term that is relevant to fundraisers in non-profit organisations unless they are running charity shops or other trading activities. However, we want to use the term in its wider marketing sense as representing those who are involved in an exchange relationship with you. You offer them something they need, and they reciprocate with something of value to you – usually, but not always, of financial value. If both parties are satisfied by these exchanges, you have the basis for a lasting and mutually beneficial relationship. Another point to consider is that involvement in reciprocal exchanges with you usually makes customers both customers and suppliers at the same time.

Let's think for a moment about what is involved in these exchanges. Our discussion of stakeholders, stemming from the flows of inputs and outputs illustrated in Figure 3.1, concentrated on financial inputs. They came from customers to private-sector organisations or from donors and funders to voluntary organisations. We argued that a big difference between organisations in the private and voluntary sectors was that outputs (products, benefits or services) went straight to paying customers in the private sector but usually to users who did not themselves pay for them in the voluntary sector (though there are, of course, exceptions to that pattern). In general, our discussion supported the distinction between a *customer*, who pays for something and may or may not use it themselves, and a *consumer*, who uses something but may not necessarily pay for it. People who go grocery shopping for their families will appreciate this distinction

But, while it is evidently of vital importance to organisational survival, financial and material support is not the only way to pay for something in an exchange. Here are some examples of typical exchange relationships in fundraising. In exchange for a project which fulfils their policy objectives, a charitable trust gives it a grant. In return for a satisfying opportunity to help, a volunteer gives their time. In exchange for a press release which will be of interest to the readers, a journalist gives a project publicity. Or, on the personal level of your career, in exchange for your energy and initiative, your manager gives you opportunities for achievement, promotion and reward. If we start to think of all of our stakeholders as customers (not just the ones who pay us or provide funding or material resources) we can start to use the exchange concept to develop long-term, mutually satisfying relationships with all of the people and organisations on whom we depend for success. The great thing is that this is as true of people inside our organisation as it is of external customers.

ACTIVITY 3.2

Think about your internal customers (e.g. your manager, a trustee, a colleague, or even someone for whom you have management responsibility) and choose an important one (ideally where you feel the relationship could be improved). Identify them in the first column of the table below. As simply as possible, describe in column 2 what you offer them in the exchange. Then, again as simply as possible, describe what you get in return from them in column 3.

On the next line, fill in columns 2 and 3 again – but this time with what you think they really want from you, and what you'd really like to get from them to help you both succeed.

1. Customer	2. What I provide	3. What I get
Current exchange		
Ideal exchange		

Take a few moments to reflect on any differences between the current exchange and what you both might really want. Below, write down three things you could do in the next month to make the exchange more mutually satisfactory.

1 ______________________

2 ______________________

3 ______________________

One result of doing this exercise might be to reveal that you need a clearer idea of precisely what it is that your customers want from you – and, indeed, that you could help them to give you a better service by being clearer to them about what you need. Asking questions, good communication, timing, and looking for feedback can help you to improve the value of your daily exchanges and your ability to work effectively with all sorts of customers inside and outside the organisation.

What other customers and suppliers can you identify? Perhaps the ones that come to mind are your service users, or the volunteers who work with your organisation. You may have found it quite difficult to identify your customers and particularly to start thinking about other employees in other parts of the organisation in this way. Moreover, it may not always appear that your colleagues see you as a customer, for example when you ask the finance section *again* for a breakdown of the payments and receipts for the last fundraising campaign. But the better the level of service they can supply you with, the more effective you will be in keeping other customers satisfied (for example trustees or senior management through timely reports, or donors and volunteers through better-researched fundraising campaigns or applications).

This brings us to one of the most powerful aspects of seeing the people you work with as customers. The quality of what you offer each other in your exchanges has a direct bearing on the ability of the entire organisation to serve its external customers. This is because the exchanges in which we participate are not isolated events, but more like links in a chain which connects all the way to the end-user (in the case of service delivery) or to donors or funders (in the case of fundraising). In one way this might seem too obvious to be worth noting, but in another it means that everyone, even those who might never meet a donor or a beneficiary, has some degree of responsibility for how well clients are helped, or donors and funders retained and developed.

Often marketing textbooks depict these relationships as a supply chain but it may be more helpful in the context in which you are working to think of these relationships as a supply network. To complicate matters further, you will often find that your various customers and suppliers can present you with competing demands or opportunities. Effective internal marketing means being able to juggle priorities to reflect the interests of the customers who have most to offer you. Figure 3.2 tries to capture the complexity of a customer/supplier network in graphic form. As you can see, the network extends through the organisation, linking suppliers to final customers through a lattice of relationships within the organisation itself. Activity 3.3 gives you the opportunity to try mapping your own relationships in this way.

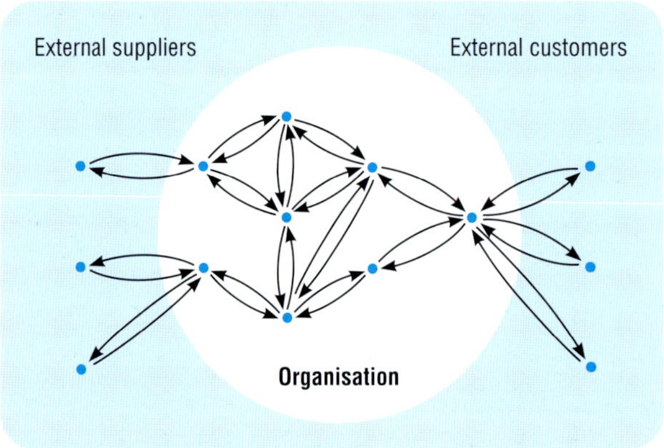

Figure 3.2 The organisation as a network of supplier–customer relationships

ACTIVITY 3.3

(a) List your main internal and external customers and suppliers.

(b) Draw the supply network showing how it relates to your role.

Thinking about your work relationships in this way helps you to understand how your work and skills contribute to the work of the organisation as a whole and its delivery to its customers. It may also give you an insight into how to serve your immediate customers better. Understanding the demands placed on them by their own customers is a good way of doing this.

That makes it all sound so simple doesn't it? But assessing and addressing the differing expectations of your various customers and suppliers can feel like a balancing act. In thinking about customers, it can be helpful to try to put yourself in their shoes. What does your job and your organisation look like to the external world? And how do your colleagues, your internal customers and suppliers, see your role and the organisation? Whether we call them stakeholders or customers, understanding, responding to, and managing their perceptions is a significant challenge in winning resources and support. It is to this we now turn by thinking about your organisation's mission, its values and how that translates into your brand or image.

3.3 BRANDING, IMAGE, MISSION AND VALUES

Many non-profit organisations are very image conscious. Campaigning organisations need to stand out by their very nature, and charities rely on the public trust generated by their reputations. Such organisations are keen to reinforce their recognition by the public. Many organisations commission research to find out the extent to which they are named by the general public when asked what charity works with a particular type of cause. Image and how the organisation is seen are inextricably linked with its potential to attract resources. But what is image and how is it developed? These days many charities are concerned to use business ideas around *branding* to manage and improve their image. A brand is defined as 'any visible sign or device used by a business enterprise to identify its goods and distinguish them from those made and carried by others' according to the *Encyclopaedia Britannica* (Media Trust, 2006). Your brand represents your organisation and sets it out as distinctive from others in the same area of operation.

BOX 3.1

BRANDING CHARITY

Many charity names (for example the Red Cross, Barnardos, the Children's Society) are over a century old. But many have under-used this valuable asset and have only recently become more proactive in the development of attractive and relevant brand propositions with which stakeholders, including donors, social policy makers, funders and staff, can identify. At the heart of the brand proposition are two key components: first the positioning or area of activity (functional component); and secondly, the values that the charity represents (symbolic component). Hence, the Red Cross defines itself in its Fundamental Principles (www.ifrc.org) as 'a leading provider of emergency help to people most in need, anywhere in the world' (functional) and, as 'impartial', 'humane', 'independent', 'unified', 'voluntary', 'neutral', and 'universal' (symbolic), (www.ifrc.org). Collectively these components describe the Red Cross brand. Significantly, it is often the symbolic component that distinguishes one charity from another when both devote themselves to a similar area of activity. For example, Tearfund, an alternative international development agency to the Red Cross, has developed a very different set of values to its competitor, focusing on a commitment to a Christian way of life and ethos.

(Adapted from Hankinson and Lomax, 2006)

Depicting charity branding as similar to positioning baked beans or crisps, with its connotations of market share and competition, may make you feel uncomfortable. You may think that this is taking voluntary organisations down an increasingly hard-nosed and commercial route. There are powerful brands in the commercial world like Coca-Cola, Ford and McDonald's but there are also powerful charity brands. Two outstanding examples are Oxfam and the International Federation of Red Cross and Red Crescent Societies. These are the kind of charities that spring to people's minds when they are thinking about donating to famine and disaster relief. They have spent time working on creating an identity that chimes with donors. Powerful brands matter even in the charity world and the reality is that voluntary organisations, for all their rhetoric of cooperation and collaboration, *are* in competition for resources. Organisations that let their image become tired, jaded and dated are also those that are unlikely to be successful in raising substantial sums of money for the cause.

ACTIVITY 3.4

Think about your own organisation. What would you say its brand was?

You may have been surprised at some of the things you started to think about. You may have considered your logo on your notepaper first, but then started to think about

> *what your organisation actually does and the particular views you have as an organisation about how it should be done.*

Your brand derives from your *mission*. In the hierarchy of purposes we looked at in the previous session the organisation's overall goal or mission is the highest level – the reason you exist. Everything else you do as an organisation flows from this – the sub-goals and objectives, the individual projects and tasks. But in essence the mission specifies the 'what' and, as Hankinson and Lomax argue in Box 3.1, the brand is created by the addition of your values – 'how' you implement your mission, what you believe is intrinsically important and distinctive about *your* approach to the work you do.

> A brand is more than just a logo or an image. It provides a first impression of your organisation and shapes the way in which the public perceives your work.
>
> (Media Trust, 2006)

The features of a successful brand (as it is often the first thing your potential donors see) are that it should:

- clearly express the charity's vision and values
- have an appeal to your target audience
- result from consistent messages, steadfast marketing efforts, good experiences and positively reinforced images
- be explicit about your needs and objectives and convey what you want from your backers
- inform those who might benefit from your services of exactly what you offer
- permeate all external and internal communications (make sure that the language and attitude of your staff reflect the charity's brand and objectives)
- feature consistently on all your materials.

Look at the examples that follow of brand images created by some charities. How successfully do they communicate what each organisation is about?

Marie Curie Cancer Care
Devoted to Life

1 Marie Curie Cancer Care

Muslim Aid
Serving Humanity

2 Muslim Aid

Patron: H.R.H. The Prince of Wales

3 Isles of Scilly Wildlife Trust

4 Deepalaya (India)

5 Caritas Internationalis

You can find brief descriptions of each organisation's role and their website addresses at the end of the session. Notice how the use of words (the 'strapline') like 'Devoted to Life' in the case of Marie Curie Cancer Care can amplify the subtle message of the visual image used.

If you work for a smaller organisation, you are possibly thinking that branding and image is all very well for those in the 'big league' but that sort of slickness is not for you. However, think about this distinction: brands may be consciously created but organisations often give off images without thinking about it. Even if you don't choose to actively manage your brand, you are still at the mercy of how you are perceived – and this can be less than flattering. In the words of the Scots poet Robert Burns:

> O wad som' Pow'r the giftie gie us
> Tae see oursels as others see us.
>
> ('To a Louse')

This, in the case of organisations, translates roughly as 'it would be good if we could stand back and see ourselves through the eyes of our donors'. How do you look to outsiders? Consider the issues in Activity 3.5:

ACTIVITY 3.5

Think about the items in the checklist below that apply to your organisation. If your organisation is large you may just want to focus on the unit where you work, but remember that your image will be affected by what the rest of the organisation does. Next to each one, write down one or two adjectives that an outsider might use to describe the impression they received.

You might, for instance, describe your office as 'messy' or your treatment of people coming to their first meeting as 'welcoming'.

Features of your organisation	Impression on an outsider
1 The appearance of your building and the places that outsiders have access to (e.g. reception areas, meeting rooms).	
2 The appearance of staff.	
3 The way someone is treated when they first come to your office or to a meeting.	
4 The way the phone is answered.	
5 The appearance and layout of your website – how easy is it to navigate and read?	
6 The speed with which enquiries are followed up (e.g. how long it takes to respond to a letter asking about joining).	
7 The appearance, accuracy and consistency of letters newsletters or leaflets produced by different parts of the organisation.	
8 The impression given by the annual report and the Annual General Meeting.	
9 The prominence and credibility of any sponsors or partners.	
10 The organisation's track record.	

Now put together a brief description of how an outsider might see you, based on the adjectives you have listed. Are there any areas where you think your organisation needs to do more work to enhance its image? Give reasons for your answer.

You may well have come to the conclusion that your organisation needs to do some work on its image. We will consider how you might go about this in the next section.

3.4 CHANGING AND DEVELOPING YOUR IMAGE

Poor images usually creep up on organisations. This is tied into the life cycle – organisations go through stages of development and typical problems seem to arise at each stage. Work by Daft (1994) suggests that there are four stages in an organisational life cycle: birth, youth, midlife and maturity.

At *birth* the energy of creating something new and the strong beliefs that the organisation's founders have in what they are doing often drive the resource-winning activities. As the organisation develops, in its *youth* stage, it finds that it needs to bring in others who were not part of the original inner circle and some formal systems and procedures for administration start to emerge. A need to develop fundraising strategies will be identified. At *midlife*, the organisation may become quite large, will have formal systems and a specialist division of labour (for example finance officers and dedicated fundraisers) operating to manuals of procedure and agreed policies. Often at this stage, managers may feel that everything is well set up and they can relax. By *maturity*, the organisation may have become set in its ways and in danger of stagnation. Decision making may be slow and centralised and image may have become a bit out of date. Here organisations can hit serious problems.

Many longer-established organisations have found that they need to change how they present themselves to the public. There are a large number of charities in the UK that were founded in the nineteenth century and which have had to work on their image as the world ethos has changed. The case study of the YWCA England & Wales (formerly known as Young Women's Christian Association) that follows (Box 3.2) illustrates some of the issues involved in how an organisation that needs to change its image goes about the process.

BOX 3.2

FROM BLUE TRIANGLE TO DANCING PINK WOMEN

The YWCA, a medium-sized charity in England and Wales, is one of the oldest women's organisations in the world. It was founded in 1855 following the efforts of Miss Emma Robarts and The Hon. Mrs Arthur Kinnaird. Miss Robarts started groups for young women who were coming to London for the first time. Mrs Kinnaird opened a hostel in Upper Charlotte Street, London for Florence Nightingale's nurses, en route to and from the Crimea. For over 140 years the organisation has worked to ensure that all women are able to take their place in society and reach their full potential.

Over the years the YWCA had developed a range of social housing for women including hostels and housing association provision, as well as many youth and community projects which supported girls and young women in realising their rights to an independent and fulfilling life. A review of the organisation's work in 1999 indicated that much of the housing provision of the YWCA no longer met the needs of young women – it was seen as old-fashioned, often in the wrong location and, moreover, the environment for social housing was changing in ways that would affect its financial viability for the organisation. The trustees therefore decided to cease this aspect of the work and concentrate on youth and community work. This change had to be undertaken in a manner consonant with the values of the organisation, which meant that no one was to be made homeless, since the needs of its client group were of primary importance. Second, staff should be treated well, and third, the organisation needed to demonstrate good stewardship of its assets. A planned communications strategy for the change was put in place. By April 2003, the organisation had changed from having over sixty housing and hostel properties to just two.

An important aspect of this change was to balance looking after the exit of staff transferring to other housing providers with the needs of the staff who were staying. In addition, research both with the public and with Members of Parliament had indicated a serious image problem in that the YWCA's public image had not kept pace with the reality and relevance of the work it does on the ground. People often saw it as an old-fashioned, stuffy charity whose remit included promoting organised religion. They also still associated the organisation with housing provision rather than as a leading provider of a range of services for young women and a campaigner on women's issues.

Some way of creating space between the 'old' YWCA and the 'new' needed to be found. A change of visual identity and new strapline was agreed as the way to do this. Everyone felt the blue triangle with the strapline 'Positive Action for Women' had associations with the old YWCA and of nineteenth-century housing, so with the help of a design firm the organisation set about developing a new visual identity.

YWCA
of Great Britain

A wide consultation exercise was undertaken involving all the stakeholders and this was managed by a steering group comprising people who represented all the different audiences of the organisation. A questionnaire which offered four logos was sent to over 1000 people and the results ultimately produced the logo and strapline below.

ywca
women changing lives

'women changing lives'

Joanna Matthews, Director of Fundraising said, 'The change has been universally loved and we have had no problems implementing it. It gives everyone a boost and an uplift, but it didn't tackle who we are or what we do. Of course repositioning is an ongoing process and sometimes incremental. We realised how much our image had changed when we won a prize for the best voluntary sector stand at the Labour Party spring conference, a real boost to our credibility.'

But the issues went much deeper than this. Having sold the properties there was a lot of capital in the bank but the YWCA also needed an ongoing revenue strategy, so the decision was taken to invest in repositioning the organisation. Joanna says, 'This has involved looking at what we do in a consistent way. Who are our key audiences? What is the competition? What are our core values? It has been an enormous learning process and there has been a lot of dialogue. The important thing has not been to do it by the book but to devise with the consultants a process that has worked for us.' This proved to be a much richer and more challenging process than was anticipated. Joanna says 'One of the tough things about importing business models into the charity sector is that it doesn't work in quite the same way. Classically in business rebranding you do your market research and design your product around it. But in the charity sector your original purpose defines the client group you work with and so you can't just decide to go with something completely new even if it might be easier to fundraise for.'

'A big learning point for us was that we had all the procedures and policies but we didn't really know how our organisation worked. We were fortunate in having money in the bank so we had time to do this properly. It has affected everything we do – absolutely every interaction with our audiences from how we describe ourselves to what we put in our literature and the kind of language we use to talk about young women.'

ACTIVITY 3.6

(a) Think about the issues raised in the case above. Note down the actions you would have to take in your own organisation to manage your brand in a similar way.

(b) What challenges would this pose for your organisation?

The issues involved in managing your brand are addressed in the checklist which follows after a brief reflection on the effort required to build and maintain a strong brand.

Kristine Kirby Webster (2002) argues:

> To be blunt, there is no shortcut, no quick answer. A strong brand is the result of good experiences; consistent messages; and positive, reinforcing images over time. Inherent in this brand strength are factors such as trust and reliability. Neither are created overnight, whether with a donor or with a consumer. It takes time and effort to create a brand image, and to make it a bankable asset. But that effort results in a brand image and association. People buy brands for the halo effect they perceive they get from it. Gucci suggests style; ... Jaguar suggests wealth; and the Red Cross suggests relief and compassion.

This cannot be achieved by quick fixes but is the result of carefully managed planning with commitment to building your brand. This involves:

- *Putting someone in charge of brand management* – This may be you as the fundraising manager or chief executive, but it needs to be someone's job to make sure that a consistent message is being put out by the organisation by reviewing all your materials including your web pages, advertisements and other communications.
- *Define your brand* – Look at your mission statement, your work and your values. The brand image must be representative of these, reinforce them and create cohesion between them. Ask questions such as: who are you, what do you do, how do you do it, and – most importantly – whom do you help?
- *Who are your competitors?* – Who else occupies the same territory? How do you compare with them? What do you do better or worse than they do? What are your donors' Unique Reasons to Give (URG)?
- *Educate the organisation about the brand* – It is vital to ensure that this is not just something thought up by the senior managers of the organisation. To be successful your brand image must permeate the whole organisation so that all employees and volunteers understand your core beliefs and values. This also means it must have the strong and explicit backing of the board members and the senior managers to be successful.
- *Make sure your marketing and communication plans support and reinforce the brand* – Ensure the strategic plan of the charity incorporates and supports the brand image at every turn. Have a house style where everything from logo and colours, to typeface and language, is consistent.
- *Let the brand drive your activity* – The brand should drive all communications, and be a carefully planned part of each communication, whether it is an appeal, a newsletter, a website, collateral materials or a special event. The brand is part of the charity's personality.

(Adapted from Kirby Webster, 2002)

3.5 IMAGE AND YOUR SERVICE USERS – SOME TENSIONS

You will recall that one of the issues Joanna Matthews raised in talking about rebranding the YWCA was 'the kind of language we use to talk about young women' and the implications that had for its fundraising. The organisation felt it needed to revisit the way it talked about its service users to avoid placing them in a subservient relationship rather than being engaged in a joint endeavour of personal change. How you talk about what you do also relates to your organisational values.

ACTIVITY 3.7

(a) What sort of image do you try to create of what you do when asking for resources?

(b) Do you present the same image to every potential donor?

(c) Do you ever have debates or arguments with others in your organisation about how to represent what you do? What issues arise from this?

Tensions can arise over the language and images used to represent the service users and activities of the organisation that derive in part from the motivations of donors to give. These motives do not always sit comfortably with an empowering approach to work with service users or those who seek to challenge stereotypes of the elderly and people with disabilities.

The whole issue about how to represent what the organisation does to potential donors and funders is a fraught one and can be the source of much soul-searching and heated debate. At its best this can mean emphasising different aspects of the organisation's work to different potential donors, and at its worst negative stereotypes of service users, hypocrisy, tension and bad working relationships between fundraisers and the rest of the organisation that can spill over into negative publicity.

Competition for funding has become very intense and some charities have resorted to shock tactics to gain the attention of potential donors, but this can have a severe backlash. Some years ago a UK animal welfare charity came under attack for featuring a large heap of dead dogs in one of its adverts to draw attention to the consequences of insufficient funding. More recently, Barnardo's, the UK charity working with disadvantaged children and young people, has come under attack for its campaign showing very young children doing things that will occur later in their lives such as taking drugs or self-harming in some way.

One advert in particular, which told the chilling tale of a young male who was raped as a child and took his own life at the age of 26, caused an outcry from groups representing parents of young people who had committed suicide. Similarly, glossy magazines have rejected advertisements from Médecins Sans Frontières, the international medical charity, that show images they regard as too shocking for their readers. The stark black and white images included a photograph of a hand with two fingers missing, and a young man with a severed arm, alongside an explanation of the charity's work.

But trying to show positive images is equally tricky. Consider the extract from *the Guardian* in Box 3.3.

BOX 3.3

NEGATIVE IMAGE

When a leading overseas aid organisation broadcast a direct response TV (DRTV) campaign earlier this year, it hoped the move would raise much-needed funds for its work. Instead the ads generated almost no response at all, resulting in a costly and disappointing exercise for the charity.

The organisation, which does not want to be named, attributes this failure to the 'good news' message conveyed by the broadcast. Instead of the usual images of starving children or beneficiaries being portrayed as 'victims', the ads had an upbeat tone and invited potential donors to help the organisation continue the good work it was doing. But in trying to avoid the clichés associated with so many charity ads, it had actually shot itself in the foot [by defeating the object of the advertisement].

'People have set ideas about poverty and the developing world; we wanted to deliver a refreshing change from the "guilt" format but people just didn't pick up the phone,' said a spokesman for the charity. 'They saw positive images so thought that the job was already done and that we didn't need their money.'

(Source: Ramrayka, 2001)

This suggests that there is no easy answer. Some advertising agencies advocate that the trick is to give positive messages but in a way that suggests that there is still more to be done. But this is not easy to do.

There are also issues about the messages given out by your organisation's name itself. As we discussed above, organisations' brand names carry a lot of meaning. But sometimes we come to see certain words in a new way as a result of changing social norms and it becomes no longer acceptable to refer to service users by the name of the original charity. One such term that is now seen as inappropriate is 'mental handicap'. When the Scottish Society for the Mentally Handicapped changed its name after much discussion to Enable Scotland, its English counterpart became Mencap. This was subsequently challenged anew as an abbreviation perpetuating an unacceptable phrase revealing what critics called an outdated attitude in the organisation. The internal debates around issues like this can be ferocious, and the external public relations fallout can be problematic. Undertaking to change the name of your organisation is not a decision to be taken lightly. People grow attached to and identify strongly with names. It may be difficult convincing people that a change of name is necessary.

It is often even harder to get agreement on a new name. Perhaps more importantly, your existing name may be well known and you risk losing this recognition and possibly causing confusion.

3.6 SUMMARY

Here is a summary of the main learning points from this session:

- In spite of its fundamental role in sustaining organisations, fundraising is often surrounded by tensions. Understanding the different internal expectations of stakeholders and customers is a step towards managing this.
- A stakeholder is any person or group that has a legitimate interest in your organisation and what it does, and the capacity to affect it. Stakeholder relationships in the non-profit sector are more complicated than those in business, as follows:
  - consumers (who use services) are usually not the same as customers (who pay for them) causing imbalance between supply and demand
  - voluntary sector organisations are held in trust by boards of trustees, not owned by shareholders or individuals
  - internal stakeholders can underestimate the status of fundraising and impose conflicting expectations on fundraisers.
- Fundraisers' professional perspectives often vary from those of their internal colleagues.
- A customer is an individual or organisation involved in a reciprocal exchange of value with a supplier. In this sense, customers are also suppliers.
- The customer/supplier relationship is as relevant to co-workers (internal customers) as it is to external customers.
- Marketing exchanges are not isolated events but part of a supply network of customers and suppliers. This means that an organisation's ability to serve its external customers relies on how well its internal customers serve each other.
- A brand is any visible sign or device used by a business enterprise to identify its goods and distinguish them from those made and carried by other brands.
- Brands have a functional component (e.g. what an organisation does) and a symbolic component (e.g. the values the organisation represents). The symbolic component is particularly useful in differentiating an organisation.

- Proactive management of your brand reduces the risk of giving off poor images inadvertently.
- Organisations need to review and refresh their images in order to remain relevant to donor needs.
- As part of how an organisation represents what it does, branding has an ethical dimension.

Brand image answers from p. 77–8:

1 Marie Curie Cancer Care provides high-quality nursing, totally free, to give terminally ill people the choice of dying at home supported by their families. Funds a number of nurses, ten hospices in the UK and medical and nursing research. http://www.mariecurie.org.uk/

2 Muslim Aid works with partners in fifty countries across Africa, Asia, Europe and the Caribbean on emergency/disaster relief as well as strategic programmes for poverty eradication that focus on education, skills training, provision of clean water, healthcare and income generation projects. http://www.muslimaid.org/

3 Isles of Scilly Wildlife Trust is responsible for managing land, conserving the islands' wildlife and their habitats, and looking after archaeological and historical remains on the islands. http://ios-wildlifetrust.org.uk

4 Deepalaya (India) works with the poor in India to provide child education, vocational training, health and community development in order to foster self-reliance. http://www.deepalaya.org/index.php3

5 Caritas Internationalis is a confederation of 162 Catholic relief, development and social service organisations working through partnership to build a better world, especially for the poor and oppressed, in over 200 countries and territories. http://www.caritas.org/

Session 4

The Ethical Context

Session 4

CONTENTS

4 THE ETHICAL CONTEXT

4.1 INTRODUCTION

Getting it right in fundraising is really important. We all know when things have gone badly wrong for we see headlines like 'Pair jailed for pocketing cancer cash' or 'Kidney charity closes after damning report'.

But how did the organisations in which these events occurred get into such messes? Generally most people undertaking fundraising activity do not set out to break the law. It happens usually because those in charge did not pay sufficient attention to the ethics of fundraising. What constitutes good practice? Fundraising thrives on innovation and new ideas to capture the interest and enthusiasm of donors and supporters. But what if innovatory approaches to fundraising take you into uncharted territory where the ethical implications are unclear? In many cases the rights and wrongs of the situation will seem self-evident. But some other situations are not so clear-cut. This session will help you to think systematically about how to approach these complex issues.

Aims and learning outcomes

The aims of the session are:

- to understand some of the ethical dilemmas involved in fundraising
- to explore the role of regulatory frameworks and codes of practice
- to examine the meaning of 'good practice' in terms of accountability, openness and trust.

After studying this session you should be able to:

- explain what is meant by ethical fundraising
- recognise some of the common ethical dilemmas involved in winning resources
- identify the good practice in your own organisation's commitment to accountability and openness – and any areas for improvement
- draw on appropriate regulatory frameworks and codes of practice in promoting good fundraising practice

This session is in three main sections and starts by examining what we mean when we talk about ethical behaviour and why this can pose so many complex problems for fundraisers. In the second section we will explore the factors that can make dealing with ethical issues tricky. The final section will suggest some ways in which you can set up systems and procedures aimed at ensuring that you abide by ethical behaviour.

4.2 ETHICS: A SLIPPERY CONCEPT?

Ethical behaviour is a major concern in many areas of our lives. We cannot turn on the radio without hearing discussions about ethical dilemmas that face people in all sorts of situations. These may include:

- purchasing dilemmas, such as whether buying furniture made from tropical hardwood perhaps contributes to the destruction of the rainforests
- individual and family decisions about whether to make use of private medicine and education
- professional dilemmas about withholding or rationing medical treatment in certain circumstances
- corporate dilemmas, such as holding investments in arms manufacture or tobacco.
- Reflection on these may prompt you to think that behaving ethically is not always easy. You may be clear that *you* think certain types of behaviour are wrong – but you will be aware that there are issues where other people hold passionate views on both sides of the debate, particularly around issues of life and death, such as euthanasia or legalised abortion.
- Ethical behaviour is about making moral judgements about what is right and what is wrong and then developing codes of practice to hold these beliefs in place and provide the basis for expressing them in action. Many ethical issues are given force by legal requirements – for example there are strict laws governing the conduct of much fundraising practice, from the handling of computer data to the regulation of house-to-house collections and raffles. But it is not just about big issues. Some other areas are not at all clear-cut and need to be decided by each organisation, developing its own view of what is acceptable according to its particular values and beliefs. Consider your reaction to the issues Activity 4.1.

ACTIVITY 4.1

Complete the following questionnaire by ticking the appropriate column.

		Never	Sometimes	Often
1	Have you taken any promotional materials such as pens, pads, badges or balloons home from work for your personal use?	❏	❏	❏

		Never	Sometimes	Often
2	Have you included personal telephone calls in your fundraising costs?	❑	❑	❑
3	Have you pretended to be out when a particularly demanding volunteer calls up to speak to you?	❑	❑	❑
4	Have you exaggerated to one potential donor or funder the extent of another donor or funder's commitment to your organisation in order to gain their support?	❑	❑	❑
5	Have you blamed the volunteers (or any one else) when things go wrong?	❑	❑	❑
6	Have you criticised your organisation to outsiders?	❑	❑	❑
7	Have you claimed credit for a success that really was the work of someone else?	❑	❑	❑
8	Have you broken a confidence in order to impress a funder?	❑	❑	❑
9	Have you done what you believed was wrong because everyone else does it?	❑	❑	❑
10	Have you told the board what it wants to hear rather than what it needs to hear?	❑	❑	❑
11	Have you taken free lunches from someone eager to associate themselves with your organisation?	❑	❑	❑
12	Have you blamed the administration when donors do not get thanked quickly?	❑	❑	❑
13	Have you bent the rules to get things done?	❑	❑	❑
14	Have you done anything you fundamentally disagreed with?	❑	❑	❑
15	Have you covered up for a colleague?	❑	❑	❑
16	Have you taken donated goods (for example at a charity shop) at a discount because you are staff?	❑	❑	❑
17	Have you got a friend tickets for a charity performance at a discount or arranged for them to meet a celebrity visitor?	❑	❑	❑
18	Have you taken donations from companies that you know run counter to your organisation's values?	❑	❑	❑
19	Have you discriminated against potential or existing staff or volunteers on the basis of age, ethnicity, sexual orientation, gender or religion?	❑	❑	❑

		Never	Sometimes	Often
20	Have you sold raffle tickets, forgotten to hand them in and kept the money?	❑	❑	❑
21	Have you manipulated the financial information to show that you have reached your targets when really you have not?	❑	❑	❑
22	Have you pretended that two different sums of money are both being used for the same project in order to free up the money for core costs?	❑	❑	❑

(Adapted from Lawton, 1998, pp. 27–8)

The point of this activity is not to demonstrate how honest and upright you are but to show the vast range of choices we face in organisational life about how we conduct ourselves. These are not easily resolved or managed.

Behaving ethically is not easy and this applies as much in voluntary and non-profit organisations as anywhere else. Some of the behaviours we listed above are illegal (like discrimination or misappropriating funds). Others, such as pretending to be out when someone calls or taking the credit for someone else's work, are not usually subject to legal sanction but instead are regarded as morally unethical. This means that ethical behaviour in fundraising is not just about doing things right legally, but also morally.

What we regard as ethical or morally right arises from our *values*: what we regard as important about how we, and the organisations where we work, ought to behave. When words like 'good', 'should' and 'ought' enter the vocabulary, it is an indication that we are in ethical territory. In essence, when we talk about values and ethical behaviour we are talking about the criteria we use in our day-to-day work to make decisions. Indeed, you may not be wholly conscious of doing this, until someone challenges your decisions and you are forced to justify them.

It is this underpinning of values that makes ethical behaviour a 'slippery concept', for values have many different sources. We have dominant values in our *society* – historical, religious, political and cultural contexts – and these in turn affect the way our *organisational* values are shaped. The latter will come from the founding stories, missions and values (Schwabenland, 2006) that subtly shape and make organisations distinctive from one another, even within the same field. We will also hold values as a *group*. We often make statements about what and who we are as a person through the organisations and associations that we join, whether they are political parties, professional bodies, religious groups, or even things like sports or fitness clubs. Similar issues apply to work groups within an organisation which may develop differing values about how things should be done. And finally, we each hold sets of *individual* values and these may connect or clash with those of the group, organisation or society.

This is tricky stuff to pick your way around and there is no getting it right all the time. Two things stand out about the issue of dealing with values. First, arguments about values are not always arguments about 'right and wrong'. One dilemma for managers is that *conflicts over values are usually conflicts between different and incompatible rights.* In many countries the issue of whether or not people should be able to hunt animals for sport is a hotly debated topic where the proponents of differing positions draw on different types of values to support their arguments. No amount of debate will produce a compromise between the two positions. Those against hunting see animals as part of a complex web of nature with 'rights' as conscious subjects of a life. Those in favour of hunting may emphasise individual human freedom to pursue sports that other people may not like but which do not harm them, the economic contribution of hunting, or the right of farmers to protect their livestock.

Second, the language in which ethical debates are conducted often creates confusion and misunderstanding. People rarely distinguish between the different types of values, behaving instead as if all values are consistent with each other, although they are not. However, we often choose to ignore this, for it is uncomfortable to realise that what is good for private individuals does not always line up with what is good and right for our work colleagues, our organisations or even political movements. Table 4.1 distinguishes some of the different sources of values.

Table 4.1 A classification of the language of values

Type of value	Examples of language used
Generalised	Good, right, ought, should
Ideological	Individualistic, collectivist, liberal, socialist
Social/political	Just, fair, free, equal, voluntary, charitable
Instrumental	Efficient, effective, appropriate, quality
'Process'	United, diverse, pluralist, in solidarity with
Behavioural	Caring, serving, tolerant, kind, sharing
Personal	Honest, in good faith, with integrity

In the voluntary and non-profit sectors we often pride ourselves on the ways in which we are true to our values and that somehow we stand on higher moral ground than so-called 'hard-nosed' commercial organisations. But in reality we all subscribe to such different values that behaving ethically is in practice bound to involve tensions and compromises.

Consider the issues raised by the cases in Activity 4.2.

ACTIVITY 4.2

Consider the cases below. What sort of ethical issues do they raise? What would you do in situations like this?

(a) A unitary national organisation has offices in three regions of the country, running local activities for members, in addition to a head office in London. There have been tensions for some time with members in one of the local offices, who actually consider themselves to be an independent charity, although the situation has been clearly explained to them several times. By chance, the national director discovers that two branch members have pretended to a funder that the branch is in fact an independent organisation and have applied for (and been granted) funding to which they are legally not entitled, as the funder's rules state that only the head office of an organisation can receive grant aid. This bid cuts across others the organisation is making nationally to the same funder and which will benefit members throughout the whole organisation. Only one bid per organisation will be accepted each year by this funder.

(b) An international aid organisation has received an appeal for help from a group of people trapped in the high mountains of one of the world's trouble spots. They are likely to be a massacred as part of an ethnic cleansing process by the dominant faction in the country. You need an all-terrain vehicle to rescue them and time is short. An offer comes in from an arms manufacturer and realistically you know that this is the best offer you are likely to get in the time available, but your organisation's ethics statement explicitly excludes accepting donations from organisations involved in any way in the arms trade.

(c) A fundraiser in a hospice for the terminally ill is asked by a nurse to visit a patient who wishes to change her will and leave all her money to the hospice because she is so grateful for the care she has received. However, her family, on learning about this, accuse both the nurse and the fundraiser of exploiting someone whose mind is befuddled by powerful drugs and therefore incapable of making a rational decision. They argue that the patient would not have made this decision to disinherit them without the pressure put on her by the self-interested actions of the hospice and its staff.

(d) The divisional manager of a charity shop network has noticed that takings have declined substantially at one shop. At first it is suspected that volunteers are not putting all the takings through the till and that some are pocketing the money. However, it emerges that the new manager is allowing the volunteers to purchase items they see when sorting the donations at a substantial discount.

Case (a) raises issues about personal values, in particular acting with integrity, and there are issues about what is good for local members in the branch versus what is good for the whole organisation. There are also issues about the legality of what the local members did. The organisation might make a short-term gain, but at the cost of damaging its reputation and future prospects for gaining grants from the funder. The chief executive in this case, after taking soundings from people who understood the funding rules, went to the funder and explained the situation. The funding was withdrawn from the local branch and the branch members went out and set up a separate organisation. A high cost to the national organisation, but it was the route the executive committee were all most comfortable with as it preserved their integrity and good name with the funder.

Case (b) illustrates the inconsistency of two different ethical positions. The first is to preserve life, which is a universal value, the second is about the integrity of the organisation and its funding sources. Here the fundraiser cannot satisfy both. In this case, after taking advice from the Institute of Fundraising, the organisation took the donation as its mission was to save life and had it refused the offer, it would have been failing to achieve its objectives.

Case (c) poses dreadful dilemmas for a fundraiser. The circumstances in which a donation is offered raise questions about whether undue influence may have been applied by a nurse to whom the patient is grateful. The fact that the patient is under the influence of powerful painkilling drugs complicates the situation. There are issues about the rights of other relatives to their inheritance and whether they might contest the will, with all the attendant costs and bad publicity for the hospice. In this case the fundraiser discussed the situation with the donor who, having discussed her wishes with her doctors, agreed to come off the painkilling drugs to ensure that her mind was unaffected and to make her will with a lawyer who was independent of the hospice.

Case (d) raises issues of clarity of expectations. If the organisation does not make explicit its policies on donated goods and the extent to which volunteers may benefit from their position as the first potential purchaser to see the goods, then this case is what results. It highlights the need to develop policies and to communicate these clearly to all staff and volunteers so that they know what is expected of them.

From this feedback you will realise that dealing with fundraising issues ethically can be difficult and that it is easy to get things wrong. As we indicated in the introduction, it is very rare for fundraisers or organisations to set out deliberately to defraud donors or their other beneficiaries. Of course, there are crooks around and some people do set out to steal from or defraud charities, but it is more usual for organisations to get into difficulties because they have not thought carefully through the issues this section discusses. The case in Box 4.1 indicates the kinds of things that may go wrong:

BOX 4.1

THE FOUNDATION FOR NEPHROLOGY LTD

The Foundation for Nephrology Ltd was established to relieve people suffering from kidney disease. It did this by way of supporting hospitals treating kidney patients and by the funding of research. The Charity Commission initiated an inquiry when concerns arose about the administration and management of the fundraising operation. The fundraisers generated an income of £4,754,842 from the public in the four years from 1 February 1996. However, only £262,650 of this total was paid over to the charity, representing only 5.5% of total fundraising income. In one accounting year no money whatsoever was passed over to the charity. The remaining 94.5% of funds raised from the public went in supporting the fundraising operation.

In the period from 1 February 1999 to 31 December 1999, the Commission found that £244,000 of donations had been collected and improperly retained by Medical Aid (UK) Ltd, the company conducting the fundraising during the relevant period.

The Commission considered that the cost structure of the fundraising was excessive in proportion to the amounts passed to the charity. Furthermore, charitable funds, which were the property of the charity and as such should have been handed over directly to the charity without any deductions, were not appropriately treated. The Commission found therefore that the fundraising operation retained charitable funds to which it had no legal entitlement. In the Commission's view, this was a clear abuse of the public's trust.

Relationship between the charity and the fundraising operation

The charity conducted its fundraising primarily through a fundraising operation controlled by the executive chairman and the financial controller of the charity. The charity and the main fundraising company, Medical Aid (UK) Ltd, shared office premises, staff, equipment and other resources and overheads. The division between the activities of the charity and the fundraising operation were not kept separate and distinct, as they should have been, and it did seem that the allocation of costs and recharging of overheads were entirely accurate.

Of control exercised over the charity and fundraising operation by the trustees

The trustees were respected medical professionals who not only determined how the income of the charity could best be applied for the relief of kidney patients, but also were responsible for administering the grants made by the charity. However, they relied upon their 'management team' of the executive chairman, who was not a member of the board or a trustee, and a financial controller to supervise, monitor and control the relationship between the charity and the fundraising operation.

The trustees had never met with the auditors of the charity and exercised limited controls over its expenditure. The management team took on responsibility for these processes and decisions, including instructing the auditors over the allocation of costs relating to fundraising in the accounts.

Both the executive chairman and the financial controller had personal financial interests in the fundraising operations. As well as their salary from the charity, they had received payments from the fundraising operation. Given that personal interest, they were placed in a position of conflict which made it entirely inappropriate for them to act on behalf of the charity in the monitoring and supervision of the fundraising activity.

The cost structure of the charity and fundraising operation included payments and benefits to the management team and their family that were regularly in excess of charitable expenditure.

As a result of interventions by the Charity Commission, after attempts to rectify the problems, the trustees recognised that they did not have the financial skills to manage the charity and it closed.

(Source: adapted from Allison, 2001)

ACTIVITY 4.3

In the case in Box 4.1, the main ethical problem was the very small amount of donated monies that actually went to fund the activities of the charity as opposed to paying fundraisers, but there were other lapses that led to the problem. List below the issues about managing fundraising from this case that would give you concern.

You may have considered the following issues:

- *The attention to accountability to the donors and beneficiaries seems to have been non-existent.*
- *The activities of the charity and the fundraising company were not sufficiently separated. In particular, the boundaries between the executive chairman's and the financial controller's roles in relation to the charity, and their personal benefits from the fundraising operation, should have given the trustees some cause for concern. This led to charitable resources being applied in support of non-charitable purposes.*
- *The trustees had not exercised a sufficient degree of control of the management of the charity and its relationship with the fundraising operations.*

This was an organisation full of good intentions, involving reputable people, yet it got into difficulties that were clearly avoidable. How does this happen? Writing about company ethical lapses in the Canadian Ethics Centre's newsletter, Mark Johnson, a Canadian corporate lawyer, observes that there is a psychology of ethical lapses (see Box 4.2).

BOX 4.2

THE PSYCHOLOGY OF ETHICAL LAPSES

Only on rare occasions will hardworking and inherently honest humans knowingly commit an act of wrongdoing. In most cases, the person commits the misdeed, at most uncertain of its propriety, while convincing himself that the act was not wrong. Consciously or unconsciously, the person rationalises the act in a number of ways with one or more of the following excuses to lower the bar of ethics and relieve his conscience.

1 **'Everybody does it.'** This provides the individual with herd immunity. If the wrongdoer has any ethical pangs about the act, then it looks like no one else did for similar acts committed by them. The logic is as follows: 'I thought that the act might be wrong, but no one else did when they did the same thing. If they all thought it was okay, then who am I to judge? Perhaps my sense of ethics is wrong and theirs are right.'

2 **'It's no big deal.'** This reasoning minimises the wrongdoing to place it within a tolerable range. The person says, 'It's really

not a big deal. Nobody will notice and if they do, nobody will care.' The wrongdoer will get away with it once and perhaps once really isn't much of a problem. The problem arises after the small acts accumulate and form a large pile of ethical lapses. An example of this would be the exaggeration of expenses or the inclusion of improper expenses to be reimbursed by the *organisation*. When the person submits his expense forms for $35 or $50, he doesn't think twice. But when all the individual bills total a large amount, there could be a problem.

3 **'The problem will go away.'** This is more applicable to acts of omission rather than acts of commission. The person responsible for fixing the ethical problem ignores it and hopes that it will disappear. Misdeeds never go away. That's like pretending a crime never occurred. If anything, the problem grows like a cancer on the company and serves as an example for others in dealing with ethical problems. Inevitably, it then comes back to the responsible individual in the form of the old Watergate inquiry question, 'What did you know and when did you know it?' The original misdeed is overshadowed by the misdeed of inaction that allowed the problem to grow.

4 **'Get along by going along.'** This rationalisation is rooted in fear. After all, humans dislike confrontation. It's only natural for people to fear confronting their colleagues or superiors. What ambitious person in their right mind would say no to his or her boss? The excuse starts with the phrase, 'It's not my job to ...' or 'I'm not going to be the one to ...' One example is the famous shredding of Enron documents by Arthur Andersen. More than any other single act, this contributed to the collapse of Arthur Andersen. Someone at Arthur Andersen gave the order *and someone followed it*. Each is as guilty as the other. The subordinates who carried out the order would probably offer up the defence that they were just following orders.

Perhaps if we imperfect humans are better able to recognise our own rationalisations for actions that trigger our ethical alarm bells and recognise this reasoning in others, we'll be led to making more ethical and ultimately better business decisions.

(Source: Johnson, 2003)

We are probably all aware of the unwillingness of most people to 'speak truth to power' for fear that it will damage their prospects in the organisation. Conflict avoidance is more common than conflict seeking in organisations, yet this leads to huge problems when minor issues are left unattended to. Good ethical policy is likely to create conflicts if it is to be effective. Expectations need to be clearly communicated, understood and owned by everyone in the organisation.

The next section now explores some issues that have been raised here about good practice and how this relates to *accountability*, *trust* and *transparency*, as these qualities are vital to sustaining your ethical fundraising efforts.

4.3 SOME COMPLICATIONS: ACCOUNTABILITY, TRUST AND TRANSPARENCY

One thing you will notice from the cases in Activity 4.2 is the concern on the part of those trying to resolve ethical dilemmas to preserve the good name of their organisation. Reputation matters and those running any organisation will feel an *obligation* to ensure that they execute their duties to maintain this precious commodity. Good name is easy to lose and hard to retain, particularly in the voluntary sector where, at times, gossip and informal networking seem to be the prevailing means of communication. This feeling of obligation to perform and to behave ethically is a key component of *accountability*, which we will now examine in some detail.

4.3.1 Accountability

We are all familiar with financial accounting and the obligations it imposes to show how money has been used within an organisation, but accountability has wider meanings. It is one of those words we use all the time, often without thinking very hard about what it implies for our resource-winning. We tend to use phrases like

> 'The buck stops here.'
>
> 'We're here to serve our users.'
>
> 'We've a responsibility to our donors.'

This indicates that along with the feeling of obligation goes a sense of *responsibility* for actions taken. In essence, accountability is a moral relationship between those who delegate authority and those who receive it. This involves accounting for that *for* which one is responsible and *to* those to whom one is responsible.

But of course, this is not as straightforward as it sounds, for accountability takes different forms depending on the quality of the relationship and the degree of *trust* between the parties to that relationship.

There are three key components to an accountability relationship:

- *Delegation* – This occurs when the management of a decision or a task is handed over to another in the expectation that they will ensure its fulfilment on your behalf. It will involve a greater or lesser degree of *discretion*.
- *Responsibility* – This is the view from the other side of the relationship – and with this, as we have observed above, goes a sense of *obligation* to ensure that a task which has been

delegated to you is implemented, and to the standards expected.

- *Legitimacy* – This accountability relationship requires a recognition on the part of those being held to account of the 'right' of those demanding such an 'account' to make that demand.

The issues of *discretion* and *obligation* in the first two components often contain differing assumptions about how they will be exercised. Although there is an expectation by those supplying the resources that you will offer accountability for the way in which you manage your resource-winning activities, this is not the same as being controlled by external agencies. In theory at least, you have the option to exercise *discretion* and choose between different policies and approaches. But the scope of that discretion will vary according to the extent to which you are *required* to be accountable. For example, a report to a major donor may be an explicit condition of receiving a grant from them. There are, however, also *proactive* or *voluntary* forms of accountability, for example when a forum is established to involve users in decisions about the development of services. There is not necessarily so intense an obligation to offer this form of accountability.

These last two issues, then, highlight that *power* lies at the heart of different forms of accountability, as some of those stakeholders to whom you are accountable have more power than others to enforce that accountability. Activity 4.4 will help you to reflect on how this affects your organisation.

ACTIVITY 4.4

Consider a recent fundraising activity in which you have been involved and identify the different stakeholders.

To whom do you consider yourself accountable in your fundraising role?

How do you offer this accountability to each set of stakeholders?

What tensions and dilemmas does this give rise to?

You may have found this raises all sorts of dilemmas for you. One of the problems is that accountability can take many different forms. A useful way of distinguishing between them is to look first at the source of pressure for accountability, then at the degree of obligation to offer that accountability and lastly at the form that accountability might take. Table 4.2 identifies these distinctions with some examples.

Table 4.2

Source of pressure	Degree of obligation	Form taken
External	Formal sanctions	e.g., Annual Report and Accounts
External	Public pressure	e.g., Media reports on activities
Internal	Voluntary obligation	e.g., Members' meeting called voluntarily

One of the problems involved in offering accountability to a range of different stakeholders in a variety of ways is the sheer complexity of doing so. You may find that one set of donors is interested in one aspect of your project and another set in quite a different one. You can be juggling all sorts of different requirements from different donors and funders and these all add to the workload as well as having resource implications.

Externally required accountability has to function on the basis of mechanisms and explicit procedures. The formal mechanisms for accounting for money and programmes often tend to override the informal mechanisms that are used to account for processes and priorities. Moreover, the request from some funders (for instance, for organisations to identify how they hold themselves accountable to other stakeholders) does not necessarily get round the problem. It can result in ritual form-filling, where service users are consulted in a mechanistic way rather than because the organisation really wants their opinions.

One reason for this concern with accountability is the need to demonstrate that resources are used to good effect. It is linked with a decline in trust in our society as relationships that rely on affective ties (such as community and friendship) have been supplanted by more instrumental one based on contractual and business relationships. It is to this issue of *trust* that we now turn.

4.3.2 Trust

There is a huge academic literature on trust and we do not propose to complicate this discussion by exploring the various definitions of the concept. For example, the extent to which *trust* differs from *confidence* is probably an arid debate unless you are a moral philosopher. Trust can be quite simply defined as having confidence in either the *competence* or the *intention* of an individual or an agency to deliver what they say they are going to. So, for example, if someone says they are going to cook your dinner tonight, you might suggest eating in a restaurant if you do not rate their cooking ability highly. This is a judgement about their competence to deliver. Or in another case, if someone you know to be unreliable promises to write an article for you next week, you might ask someone else as well because you suspect that the first person will not deliver on time.

In recent years a decline in public confidence or trust in a wide range of institutions in our society has been charted and charities have not been immune from this. According to research carried out for nfpSynergy, a UK think-tank focusing on not-for-profit issues, there are concerns in the public's mind about how charities spend their money. The extract in Box 4.3 sets out their findings.

BOX 4.3

CHARITIES HIT BY DOUBTS

More than a quarter of Britons say they do not give to charity because of concerns that the money does not reach those who most need it [...] More than 75% of people think levels of giving are affected by concerns about how the money is spent, the findings suggest. Twenty-seven per cent of those questioned said it was a main reason they did not donate to charities, with 50% saying it was probably one of the main reasons why other people did not do so.

Although attitudes varied little according to respondents' social class or gender, more than a third of those aged over 55 said that where the money went was a concern for them.

The survey, by the not-for-profit think-tank nfpSynergy, does show a higher level of trust in charities than in government or companies. But it indicates there is little public understanding of how many charities feel they need to operate in the modern age.

Of more than 2,000 people consulted, about 32% did not think charities were justified in spending a proportion of donations on fundraising so that income increased in the future. Twenty-five per cent did not want any donation spent on attracting long-term supporters. Even 23% of those who regularly donated to charity through a standing order thought that investing in fundraising was unacceptable.

[...]

The researchers also questioned separately more than 200 members of the houses of parliament. About 60% of MPs and 34% of peers agreed that fundraising should be closely regulated.

However, Joe Saxton, director of nfpSynergy, says: 'The problem is how the money is spent, rather than how it is raised.

'The public needs to understand how charities now work and to have the confidence that the money is being spent to good effect. To pick out fundraising as the way to solve the supposed crisis in charities is not the way forward.'

Despite this, the survey results do suggest that direct mail appeals and street fundraising are the two activities that most irritate people about charities. High salaries and high administration costs also cause resentment.

Lindsay Boswell, chief executive of the Institute of Fundraising, urges charities to tell supporters where the money goes. 'There is no other way to increase transparency and education than through charities being more open and honest with supporters and donors,' he says.

A spokesman for the National Council for Voluntary Organisations says: 'Contrary to popular belief, only 5.5% of charities' total expenditure is spent on fundraising and publicity. We are happy to work with partners in the sector to tackle misconceptions and negative perceptions the public has about charities.'

(Source: *Guardian*, 2002)

It seems from this that a major concern of the public when asked is to know how the money they donate is spent. How can they trust charities to do what they say they are going to do? Here it will be helpful for you to reflect on the factors that influence you to decide whether or not to place your trust in an institution.

ACTIVITY 4.5

(a) Which of these do you trust most? Put a score beside each of the following from 1 to 5 according to how much you trust the institution/group, with 5 being the most highly trusted.

Army

Politicians

Journalists

Church

Charities

Doctors

(b) What factors influenced your choices of the most highly trusted and why did you score others lower?

You have probably been strongly influenced by negative publicity about the institutions or groups at the bottom of your list. Certainly, the media loves a good 'bad news' story and the occasional headline about fraud or excessive fundraising costs can have a disproportionate effect in denting public confidence in charities. You may also be influenced by personal experience, but most people tend to form their judgements based on what they read or hear from the media. Many organisations are very concerned therefore when negative publicity arises and do their best to prevent or counteract it.

Sargeant (2001) suggests that to build trust in charities, donors need to get feedback on how their money is used. This links back to our discussion about accountability. Donors' needs for feedback arise precisely because there is a desire to ensure delivery of the charity's work to high ethical standards. Lack of trust will mean that these demands are stepped up and enforced by increasing amounts of statutory regulation. So what can charities do to ensure that they do not become enmeshed in ever tightening demands for evidence of performance and probity? This brings us to the third complicating factor, *transparency*.

4.3.3 Transparency

This essentially is the idea that one way of building trust and being accountable is to ensure that the activities of the organisation in collecting and disbursing donations stand up to public scrutiny and that there is nothing hidden that the organisation is unwilling to reveal. This sounds straightforward enough, but does not allow for the damaging media coverage that can follow the release of potentially controversial information. For example, the leading UK children's charity the NSPCC found itself the subject of hostile media coverage in 2000 when its Annual Report revealed that it spent £20m out of expenditure of £75m on 'public education' and campaigning in 1999/2000. While a perfectly legitimate expenditure in terms of the organisation's strategy to achieve its mission, this was seized on as a waste of donors' money by journalists keen to peddle a simplistic version of how the charity should be operating.

This case highlights the challenge charities face in explaining to donors the real complexities of how they work. The Institute of Fundraising's code on Transparency and Accountability in Fundraising emphasises the responsibility of charities to be able to explain how their organisations and the voluntary sector in general operate to donors, beneficiaries, the public and the media (Institute of Fundraising, 2006a). An important, and influential, audience for such information are the staff, trustees and volunteers of the organisation itself. A group of UK charities have formed what is known as the ImpACT (Improving Accountability, Communication and Transparency) coalition to work together to increase public understanding of the work and values of the charity sector. One of the resources they have created is a template for organisations to brief their staff and volunteers to be able to give consistent answers that build understanding about the charity, and refute inaccurate media coverage about issues such as fundraising costs and methods. (ImpACT Coalition, 2006).

While proactive honesty and transparency with accurate and open reporting by means of annual reports, promotional material and newsletters to members and so on is vital, there has also to be careful consideration of the likely impact in publicly owning up to mistakes and failings. The best way to avoid mistakes is to develop frameworks and codes of practice for ethical behaviour that will enable you to consider carefully any new situation within your own developed guidelines. It is for this reason that many organisations invest time and effort in seeking to make their ethics policies as sound as possible. It is to these issues that the next section turns.

4.4 GOOD PRACTICE: HOW TO KEEP ON THE RIGHT SIDE OF THE LAW

One way many organisations seek to address problems like this is to set standards for ethical behaviour by developing, or adopting, an ethics statement or policy which can then act as a framework for decision making. Formalising the process, rather than just relying on our individual moral instincts, means that it is easier to make, and justify, reliable decisions in complicated situations. As Rosen (2005) argues, 'by following a code of ethics and taking a deliberative approach to decision-making, fundraising professionals will be able to make the best possible choice even when faced with no clear correct answer and will be in a better position to justify that decision to the organisation's stakeholders' (p. 176)

What does this mean in practice? Here are some guidelines for developing an approach to managing ethics in a fundraising or campaigning context:

- *Establish a written ethics policy* – If your organisation does not have one already, then create one for your team with the participation of every member. Discuss potential issues and agree on acceptable actions and behaviours.
- *Set an example* – Do the organisation's policies accurately reflect the way the work is done? If colleagues or subordinates see their manager breaking the rules or codes of practice, then there is little incentive for them to conform.
- *Instruct by means of case studies* – At team days or training events, discuss scenarios which raise dilemmas for your fundraising such as from whom to accept donations.
- *Reward ethical performance* – If you discover that a team member made good a lapse by apologising to a donor or reviewing how work is done, then that behaviour should be rewarded. The corollary, of course, is that unethical behaviour should not be tolerated. This type of discipline can be unpleasant, but it is necessary if you wish to run your organisation or section as a consistently ethical environment.
- *Encourage social responsibility* – Try to help your staff and volunteers to see how what they do contributes to the values of the organisation. Allow them to learn more about what you and similar organisations do and encourage them to get involved.

The problem with an approach like this is that it implies that implementation of such policies can be conducted in isolation from other competing pressures on the organisation. In reality there has to be a balance and inevitably errors of judgement will be made and, as we indicated in Activity 4.2, sometimes there may be no clear-cut 'right' decision.

Another important ethical territory concerns the ethos of 'whistle-blowing' – individuals exposing wrongdoing in their organisation. The complications that can arise from this are illustrated in Box 4.4.

BOX 4.4

DIVERTING FUNDS

John was in charge of a holiday home in the North West run by a charity. It provided breaks for disabled children. He and other colleagues were worried that the Chief Executive had given a large building contract to a local firm, which now appeared to be doing extensive works on the Chief Executive's home. The staff felt sure this private work was being paid for under the charity contract.

John and the other staff were told that someone had sent an anonymous letter to the trustees alerting them to these suspicions. The trustees, who were local worthies, refused to look into the matter because the report was anonymous. This led some staff to think that the trustees were complacent, and that anyone who did speak up could be dismissed.

We advised John to write to the trustees explaining why the staff suspected misconduct, indicating that while they might be mistaken, their morale would suffer unless the matter was investigated.

John followed our advice and checked his draft letter with *Public Concern at Work*. The trustees assured John that he would suffer no adverse consequences and that they would look into the matter. They then conducted an inquiry with the co-operation of the Charity Commission into the building contracts. As a result action has been taken against the Chief Executive. The trustees have been true to their word and have been very supportive toward John, who has suffered no adverse consequences at all.

(Source: Public Concern at Work, 2003)

ACTIVITY 4.6

How would you manage the (real) situation in Box 4.4 if it was drawn to your attention?

It seems that there was a failure of sound management practice. In essence 'whistle-blowing' means acting after a situation has already become very serious. You might think it would have been better to prevent this situation arising in the first place by setting proper standards of behaviour and building authorisations procedures into the organisation's financial regulations to ensure that staff do not face such dilemmas.

All professions – including fundraising – have ethical codes by which their members abide as a badge of their professionalism. Professions such as the law and medicine regard it as essential to their independence (and duty of care to clients or patients) that they regulate themselves through such codes of practice rather than being subject to external state control (while, of course, staying within the law). Fundraising is no exception to this, and the Institute of Fundraising in the UK sets out extensive guidelines for all aspects of fundraising practice in its regularly updated *Codes of Fundraising Practice* (Institute of Fundraising, 2006a), from acceptance and refusal of donations to the use of chain letters as a fundraising technique. (If you are not in the UK, you may also find that there is similar guidance for your own country available from the appropriate regulatory body for charities in your part of the world.)

As part of the drive to improve and sustain public trust in charities, in 2006 the Institute of Fundraising was complemented by the Fundraising Standards Board in the UK, an independent membership organisation which is meant to provide the public with a single point of contact for accountability in fundraising, just as the Institute provides a lead to the fundraising industry. Members sign up to an explicit 'Fundraising Promise' and commit themselves to having a complaints procedure in place to deal with any lapses in how they treat donors. Working closely together, the intention is that any issues which present themselves to the public-facing Fundraising Standards Board can then be fed back into the Institute of Fundraising's continuously improving *Codes of Fundraising Practice.*

Codes of practice are not limited to national bodies. In an increasingly international fundraising environment, networks of organisations across borders are finding it necessary to align themselves to common standards. The basic framework of good practice as agreed by twenty-four countries in October 2006 is spelt out in Box 4.5, an extract from the International Statement of Ethical Principles in Fundraising.

BOX 4.5

FIVE UNIVERSAL PRINCIPLES

Five important principles for acting as a fundraiser:

HONESTY: Fundraisers shall at all times act honestly and truthfully so that the public trust is protected and donors and beneficiaries are not misled.

RESPECT: Fundraisers shall at all times act with respect for the dignity of their profession and their organisation and with respect for the dignity of donors and beneficiaries.

INTEGRITY: Fundraisers will act openly and with regard to their responsibility for public trust. They shall disclose all actual or potential conflicts of interest and avoid any appearance of personal or professional misconduct.

EMPATHY: Fundraisers will work in a way that promotes their purpose and encourage others to use the same professional standards and engagement. They shall value individual privacy, freedom of choice, and diversity in all its forms.

TRANSPARENCY: Fundraisers stimulate clear reports about the work they do, the way donations are managed and disbursed, and costs and expenses, in an accurate and comprehensible manner.

(Institute of Fundraising, 2006c)

The case in Box 4.4 clearly breaches the principles of Integrity and Transparency as set out above.

ACTIVITY 4.7

Consider what an ethical fundraising policy for your organisation might look like.

(a) What are the key values of your organisation? – these may be in your constitution or set out in your mission and vision statement.

(b) Map out the areas where you think ethical problems could arise for you – this may be around from whom to accept donations, how fundraising is organised or the way in which volunteers participate in the process.

(c) What issues arise about accountability, trust and transparency?

(d) Do you have an ethical fundraising policy in your organisation – if yes what does it contain? If no, what do you think it should contain?

(e) Are there any aspects of the Five Universal Principles in Box 4.5 above where you fall short?

(f) If so, what can you do to address these problems?

Every set of responses to this exercise will be particular to each organisation. The important thing for you as someone involved in fundraising is that you start to become aware of the ethical issues involved in fundraising and take steps to ensure that your practice conforms to the highest possible standards.

4.5 SUMMARY

Here is a summary of the main learning points from this session:

- Ethical behaviour is about making moral judgements about what is right and what is wrong and then developing codes of practice to hold these beliefs in place and provide the basis for expressing them in action.
- What we regard as ethical or morally right arises from our *values*: what we regard as important about how we as individuals, and the organisations where we work, ought to behave.
- Values have a number of different sources: dominant values in society; organisational values connected to mission and purpose; group values from our affiliations to others; and individual values which may connect or clash with those of the group, organisation and society.
- Conflicts over values are usually conflicts between different and incompatible rights.
- The language in which ethical debates take place often creates confusion as it assumes that all values are consistent with each other.
- Apart from the rare case of fraud or dishonesty, ethical lapses tend to occur because organisations have not thought through their policies thoroughly. Expectations need to be clearly communicated, understood and owned by everyone in the organisation.
- Accountability is a moral relationship between those who delegate authority and those who receive it. It has three key components:
  - delegation (handing over the management of a task or decision to another, involving discretion)
  - responsibility (an obligation felt on the part of the delegate)
  - legitimacy (the recognition by those held to account of the right of those demanding the account).
- Power lies at the heart of different forms of accountability.
- Trust is having confidence in either the competence or the intention of an individual or an agency to deliver what they say they are going to. One way of developing trust from donors is to provide feedback on how their money is used.
- Transparency involves ensuring that the organisation and its activities stand up to public scrutiny and that there is nothing hidden that it is unwilling to reveal.
- Effective management of ethics in an organisation involves the following principles:
  - establish a written ethics policy
  - set an example
  - instruct by means of case studies
  - reward ethical performance
  - encourage social responsibility.

- In some situations individuals may have to expose wrongdoing in their own organisations ('whistle-blowing').
- A mark of a profession (such as fundraising) is to develop, uphold and police its own ethical codes. While being no less committed to the law than any other group of citizens, professionals see self-regulation as a more flexible and authentic way of managing ethical lapses than being regulated by external statutory control.
- Five Universal Ethical Principles in fundraising are:
  - Honesty
  - Respect
  - Integrity
  - Sympathy
  - Transparency

REFERENCES

Allison, R. (2001) 'Kidney charity closes after damning report', Society (supplement) *Guardian* May 17th.

Arts Professional (2007) Recruitment Advertising, Issue 137, January pp. 17–18.

Caritas Internationalis [online], http://www.caritas.org/ (Accessed 5 February 2007).

Daft, R. (1994) *Management,* 3rd edition, Forth Worth: Dryden Press.

Hankinson, P. & Lomax, W. (2006) 'The effects of re-branding large UK Charities on staff knowledge, attitudes and behaviour', *International Journal of Nonprofit and Voluntary Sector Marketing*, vol.11, pp. 193–207.

ImpACT Coalition (2006) 'Asking for It – Honest Answers to Tough Questions: The essential Q&A for all charities' [online], http://www.ncvo-vol.org.uk/impACT/?id=1272 (Accessed 5 February 2007).

Institute of Fundraising (2006a) *Codes of Fundraising Practice* [online], London, Institute of Fundraising, http://www.institute-of-fundraising.org.uk (Accessed 5 February 2007).

Institute of Fundraising (2006b) *The Good Fundraising Guide: Where to start ...* [online], London, Institute of Fundraising, http://www.institute-of-fundraising.org.uk/documents/good_fundraising_guide.pdf (Accessed 5 February 2007).

Institute of Fundraising (2006c) *International Statement of Ethical Principles in Fundraising* [online], London, Institute of Fundraising, http://www.institute-of-fundraising.org.uk/documents/Statement%20of%Ethical%20Principles%20in%20Fundraising%2016%20October%2020061%pdf (Accessed 5 February 2007).

Johnson, M. (2003) 'The Psychology of Ethical Lapses', *Management Ethics*, Winter, p. 2, Canadian Centre for Ethics and Corporate Policy [online], http://www.ethicscentre.ca (Accessed 15 July 2003).

Kirby Webster, K. (2002) 'Branding the Non-Profit', The Canterbury Group Ltd [online], http://www.brandchannel.com/images/papers/Non_profit.pdf (Accessed 5 February 2007).

Lawton, A. (1998) *Ethical Management for the Public Services*, Buckingham, Open University Press.

Media Trust 9 (2006) *Media Trust 2002 Charity Branding (Online Guide)* [online], http://www.mediatrust.org/ (Accessed 5 February 2007).

Professional Fundraising (2007) Recruitment Advertising, January, pp. 17–21.

Public Concern at Work (2003) 'Maintaining Confidence' [online], http://www.pcaw.co.uk/help_individ/maintaining_con.html (Accessed 5 February 2007).

Ramrayka, L. (2001) 'Charities struggle to find right balance with ad campaigns', *GuardianUnlimited* 15 June [online], http://www.society.guardian.co.uk/publicrelations/story/0,,507035,00.html (Accessed 5 February 2007).

Rosen, M.J. (2005) 'Doing well by doing right: A fundraiser's guide to ethical decision-making', *International Journal of Nonprofit and Voluntary Sector Marketing*, vol. 10, pp. 175–81.

Sargeant, A. (2001) *Report on Public Confidence in Charities for the Charities Aid Foundation*, London, CAF.

Schwabenland, C. (2006) *Stories, Visions and Values in Voluntary Organisations*, Corporate Social Responsibility Series, Aldershot, Ashgate.

Voluntary Service Overseas (2006) *Job Description – Fundraiser Zambia* (Volunteering Information Sheet), London, VSO.

ACKNOWLEDGEMENTS

Grateful acknowledgement is made to the following sources for permission to include material within this book:

Grateful acknowledgement is made to the following sources:

Cover Image: © Digital Vision / Getty Images;

Text

Box 1.1: Courtesy of Durham Cathedral; Courtesy of Daryl Upsall Consulting Limited; Courtesy of Canterbury City Council; Courtesy of The Drake Music Project; Courtesy of VSO; *Activity 4.1:* Lawton, A. (1998) *Ethical Management for the Public Services*, Open University Press, McGraw-Hill Education; *Box 4.1:* 'Foundations for Nephrology Ltd', Charity Commissions for England and Wales. Crown copyright material is reproduced under Class Licence Number C01W0000065 with the permission of the controller of HMSO and the Queen's Printer for Scotland; *Box 4.2:* Johnson, M. 'The Psychology of Ethical Lapses', in Management *Ethics,* Winter 2003, EthicsCentre.ca; *Box 4.3:* Benjamin, A. 'Charities hit by doubts', The Guardian, 11 December 2002. Copyright © Guardian News and Media Ltd 2002;

Illustrations

Pages 77–8: Marie Curie Cancer Care; Muslim Aid; The Isles of Scilly Wildlife Trust; Deepalaya (India) and Caritas; *Page 81:* The Young Women's Christian Aid;